MOTOR VEHICLE AND ROAD USER STUDIES

9 m

12 m

24 m

38 m

15 m

55 m

18 m

21 m

D1514521

COLOURPOINT
EDUCATIONAL

cea

Rewarding Learning

EAMONN McPOLIN

ISBN: 978 1 906578 31 2

First Edition
Fifth Impression

Layout and design: April Sky Design
Printed by: GPS Colour Graphics Ltd

COLOURPOINT
EDUCATIONAL

Colourpoint Educational
An imprint of Colourpoint Creative Ltd
Colourpoint House
Jubilee Business Park
21 Jubilee Road
Newtownards
County Down
Northern Ireland
BT23 4YH

Tel: 028 9182 0505
Fax: 028 9182 1900
E-mail: sales@colourpoint.co.uk
Web site: www.colourpoint.co.uk

The Author

Eamonn McPolin graduated from St Mary's University College Belfast with a B.Ed Hons in Technology and Design. He wrote the GCSE MVRUS Scheme of Work for CCEA (for first teaching in 2009) and is a Principal Examiner for GCSE MVRUS for CCEA. He has seven years experience teaching the subject and is currently MVRUS Head of Department in St Mark's High School, Warrenpoint.

Acknowledgments

Thanks must go to a number of people for their help, support and encouragement with the production of this book. Firstly to my wife Aisling, our young family, and my mother and father for all their support, understanding and encouragement. A special word of thanks to Alan Hawthorne (MVRUS Chief Examiner, CCEA) and Cathal McKeever (former DOE Senior Road Safety Education Officer) for their advice and support regarding the content of this book; Donna Finlay (CCEA) for the opportunity to produce this material; and to Rachel Irwin at Colourpoint for her guidance and encouragement throughout the writing process.

Picture credits

Mark Allen: 21

DVA: 50

Ford Company: 60 (top right, second from bottom)

Richard Foreman: 35

Harstook: 60 (top left)

Alan Hawthorne: 18, 22 (top and middle), 24 (bottom), 58 (top), 62 (left), 63 (top right, bottom left)

Highway Code: 6, 8, 9, 10 (bottom right), 11 (bottom right), 14, 17, 24 (top), 39 (bottom), 40

iStockphoto: 3, 19, 23 (bottom), 25, 26, 27, 28, 29, 33 (bottom), 34, 35 (bottom), 38, 39 (top), 42 (left), 46, 58 (bottom left), 60 (fourth from bottom), 61 (bottom), 63 (bottom right), 71, 72, 73, 74, 76, 80, 81

Rachel Irwin: 10 (top right), 14 (top and bottom middle), 86

Malcolm Johnston: 13 (top right), 14 (top right), 22 (bottom), 23 (top), 37, 53, 55, 57 (top), 60 (bottom), 61 (top), 64, 79 (bottom), 82

Norman Johnston: 57 (bottom), 58 (bottom right), 79 (right), 82

Wesley Johnston: 62 (right), 63 (top left, middle), 65

Richard Niewiroski Jr: 57 (middle)

NTEC: 66

Shutterstock: 32, 36, 42 (right), 47

CONTENTS

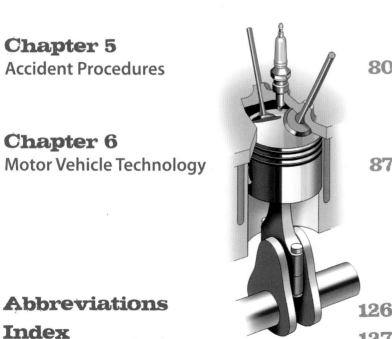

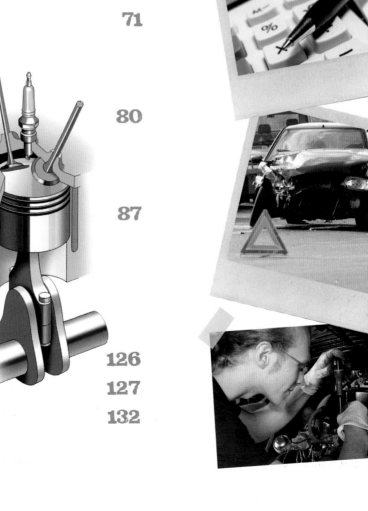

FOREWORD

FOREWORD

Having been involved in Road Safety Education for more than 33 years I welcome wholeheartedly the publication of this book. The problem of road safety generally is one that virtually all of us have to face on a daily basis and sometimes with tragic consequences. Government Departments, Police and other Road Safety Agencies spend much time and effort dealing with the problem through education, publicity, enforcement and engineering methods. These efforts have met with a significant degree of success when one compares the fatality figures with those of earlier years. However, one has only to listen to the media to realise that tragedies still take place on our roads on a far too regular basis.

It is widely accepted that education has a major role to play in influencing attitudes and ultimately behaviour on our roads. For a number of years a GCSE in Motor Vehicle and Road User Studies (MVRUS) has been available in Northern Ireland. This has all grades status and is a serious attempt to introduce positive road user behaviour to a post primary age range, which is particularly vulnerable as drivers of either two or four wheel vehicles.

I have known Eamonn McPolin, the author of this book, since he commenced teaching the subject several years ago in St Mark's High School, Warrenpoint. He approached his teaching in a most methodical way and impressed me with his imaginative use of existing resources and indeed the production of new materials, such as student workbooks. As a consequence I asked Eamonn to speak at a Post Primary Conference in Craigavon. His contribution was described by many as 'inspirational' and there is no doubt that it helped to motivate teachers in the delivery of MVRUS in their own schools.

I am well aware of the volume of work which has gone into the production of this book. By the very nature of its diverse content, the subject of MVRUS has relied upon a wide range of resources and, very often, the teacher's own initiative. This publication has been written specifically for the recently amended Specification. It covers each of the six theory sections individually, is presented in a clear and concise manner, and has a wealth of colourful illustrations. I have no doubt that it will make a highly valuable contribution to classroom teaching and will be welcomed by all in that sector of education.

I am both delighted and honoured to write this brief foreword. During my years in road safety education I was fortunate to meet a great many highly committed and enthusiastic subject teachers. Eamonn Mc Polin ranks up there with the best of them and I feel sure that his work with this book will bear the fruit that it so richly deserves.

Cathal Mc Keever MBE
Former DOE Senior Road Safety Education Officer

Chapter One

VEHICLE CONTROL AND ROAD USER BEHAVIOUR

THE HIGHWAY CODE

The Highway Code is the most important book available to the road user. This book identifies the legal requirements and is well illustrated with drawings to explain the correct procedures to be followed while on the road. The main areas of the book look at:

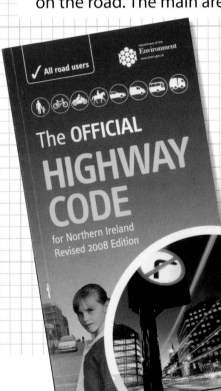

- Seat belt regulations
- Braking and stopping distances
- Correct procedures for overtaking
- Correct procedures at roundabouts
- Correct procedures when reversing
- Motorway driving
- Breakdowns and emergencies
- Road works
- Cycling requirements
- Animal regulations
- Speed limits
- Road signalling
- Signals by authorised personnel
- Traffic signs & road markings
- Vehicle markings
- Hazard warning plates

If there were no laws and rules for using the roads motorists could do whatever they wanted. This scenario would lead to more deaths, accidents, congestion and very frustrated motorists. Police and penalties both implement the law, disciplining motorists' behaviour on the roads to improve all road users' safety. The *Highway Code* clearly identifies the need for rules for all classes of road user – pedestrians, cyclists, motorcyclists, motorists, agricultural vehicles and horse riders. Each road user's mode of transport is different and therefore requires specific rules and behaviour.

The *Highway Code* is designed to prepare learner drivers for the road. It is also a book of rules that all motorists should refer to for advice on correct road procedures and manoeuvres. It provides the opportunity for even experienced motorists to compare their driving skills or habits to what the code actually recommends.

On passing the test, drivers are legally required to display 'R' Plates for one year and drive at a restricted speed limit of 45 mph.

The HIGHWAY CODE is designed to prepare learner drivers for the road

The driving test consists of two parts: a computerised theory element, testing the candidate's knowledge of the *Highway Code*; and a practical driving test monitored by a qualified driving examiner, who is usually based at each local Driver and Vehicle Agency (DVA) office or Ministry of Transport (MOT) centre. Candidates must pass the theory element before taking the practical test. The test is designed to examine learners on their knowledge of vehicle manoeuvres and road awareness. On passing the test drivers are legally required to display amber 'R' Plates for one year and drive at a restricted speed limit of 45 mph. In England drivers do not have to display any plates after passing the driving test, nor is there any speed restriction. However, drivers sometimes choose to display green 'L' or 'P' Plates to make other road users aware that they are new to driving unsupervised or on a pass plus scheme. In both Northern Ireland and England if drivers receive six penalty points in their first two years of driving they will automatically have to re-sit the driving test.

Road Signs

You see various traffic signs every day as you travel on the road. The signs are different colours, sizes and shapes, each with a specific meaning, direction or warning to help motorists use the roads safely. Therefore it is important to take note and obey each sign as you encounter it. The table below summarises the various types of traffic signs.

Type	Shape	Colour	Meaning
Prohibition Sign	○	Red Circle	What you must NOT do
Positive Instruction	●	Blue Circle	What you must do
Warning Sign	△	Red Triangle	Warns of possible danger
Direction Sign	M2	White Print Blue Background	Gives directions on motorways
Direction Sign	Newry	White Print Green Background	Gives directions on primary routes
Direction Sign	Burren ↑	Black and White	Gives directions on non-primary routes
Information Sign		Blue and White Yellow and Black Black and White	Gives information

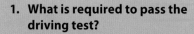
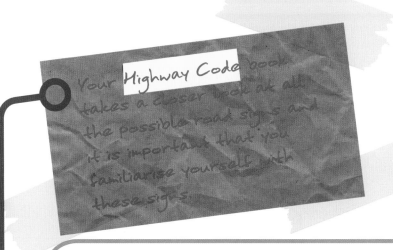

Your Highway Code book takes a closer look at all the possible road signs and it is important that you familiarise yourself with these signs.

1. **What is required to pass the driving test?**

2. **Name two legal requirements for motorists after passing the driving test.**

3. **What penalty is imposed if a restricted driver receives six penalty points in his or her first two years after passing the driving test?**

4. **List two pieces of advice you might give to a young driver who has just passed the driving test.**

5. **Study the traffic signs in your *Highway Code* book. Describe each of traffic signs below by their type, shape, colour and meaning.**

1
2
3
4

5
6
7
8
9

10
12
13
14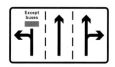

15
16
17
18
19

20

THINK

Take a look at your local newspapers to see if you can find any articles or notices of young drivers convicted for breaking the law. Cut them out and stick them in your folders under the title: 'Young drivers breaking the law on local roads'.

Signalling

Signalling, obeying signals from signs and authorised personnel form part of everyday driving. It is important that all drivers signal to inform others of their intentions. This reduces the risk of an accident. Similarly, it is important that all road users understand and obey any signals shown on signs, both for their own safety and for the safety of others.

In towns and cities traffic lights are the main signals. Driving into a strange town or city can be a daunting task if you are not sure where you are going, so leave early, take your time and drive carefully. On carriageways and motorways you must be aware of electronic signs and signals for speed limits, directions, weather conditions, diversions and often road works.

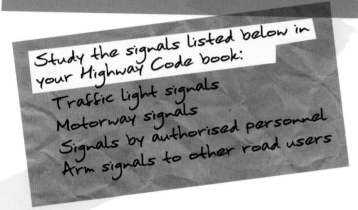

Study the signals listed below in your Highway Code book:
- *Traffic light signals*
- *Motorway signals*
- *Signals by authorised personnel*
- *Arm signals to other road users*

Signals given by authorised persons

When driving on the roads there are three main groups of people whose signals we must obey. They are the:

- Police (PSNI)
- Driver and Vehicle Agency Enforcement Officer (DVA Enforcement Officer)
- Customs and Excise Officers

When might the Police signal?

- At a road check point
- To ease traffic flow
- At an accident scene
- To divert traffic
- At large events

Stop

Traffic approaching from behind

Traffic approaching from both front and behind

Traffic approaching from the front

To beckon traffic on

From the side

From the front

From behind

TO BECKON TRAFFIC ON = TO CALL TRAFFIC TOWARDS

DVA Enforcement Officers drive marked vehicles similar to those belonging to the traffic police. To get your attention they will flash amber lights. If these lights flash from the front they are signalling that you should follow them to a safe location to stop. If these lights flash from behind they are signalling that you should pull over. Customs and Excise Officers also use signals to stop or direct vehicles to the hard shoulder at fuel fraud checkpoints, usually found on main roads. These officers have the authority to fine drivers and impound their vehicles if they are found to be using illegal fuel.

A 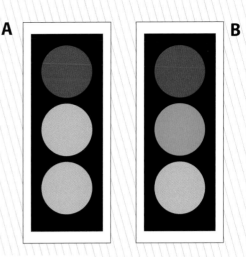 B

Primary and secondary signals

Primary light signals refer to the traffic lights that you are waiting at. If you can see further traffic light signals ahead these are secondary light signals.

The pictures (right) show the correct order for the way traffic lights work:
A. Stop
B. Stop – Do not pass until green shows
C. Go
D. Stop

C 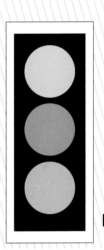 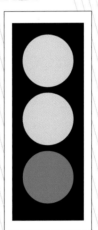 D

Signals given by drivers and others

When driving, you must remember to signal by using your indicators to tell other motorists, pedestrians, motorcyclists, cyclists, agricultural vehicles and horse riders what you intend to do or where you intend to go. You have to remember that other road users are watching for your signals at road junctions and roundabouts. Failure to signal can cause other road users to become frustrated or misjudge your intentions. In the event that your lights and indicators should fail while driving it is important that you use the following arm signals (right) instead.

I intend to move out to the right or turn right

I intend to move in to the left or turn left

I intend to slow down or stop

I intend to move in to the left or turn left

I intend to move out to the right or turn right

I intend to slow down or stop

11

Each set of road markings has a specific meaning. Some motorists ignore road markings because they simply do not understand what they mean. This could lead to serious consequences, either in the form of an accident or penalty points being awarded to the motorist because of dangerous driving.

Road Markings

All road markings have different meanings and there are two main colours used on roads – white and yellow. White is used most and found on all roads. Yellow is mainly used to indicate restrictions, such as those regarding parking and loading.

Your *Highway Code* book looks at Road Markings in more detail. It is important that you investigate these further.

Give way to traffic on a major road

Give way to traffic from right at roundabout

Give way to traffic from right at mini-roundabout

Stop line on most roads

No waiting at any time

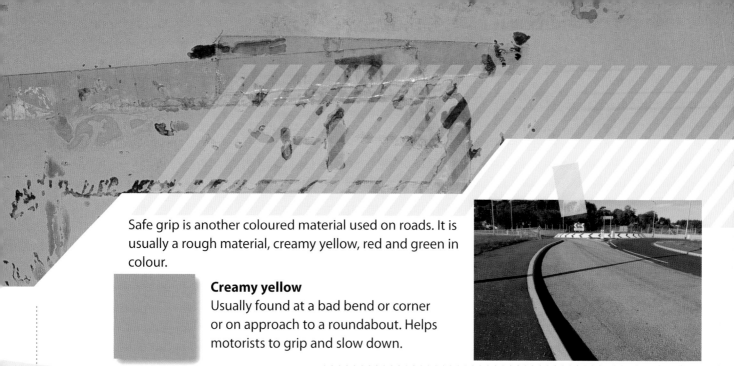

Safe grip is another coloured material used on roads. It is usually a rough material, creamy yellow, red and green in colour.

Creamy yellow
Usually found at a bad bend or corner or on approach to a roundabout. Helps motorists to grip and slow down.

Green
Usually found on cycle tracks.

Red
Usually found in built up or residential areas to indicate a speed limit of 30 mph.

Road Studs

To assist drivers on motorways at night, road studs were introduced to help motorists identify their road position more easily. Each colour of stud marks a specific position.

- **Amber** – marks the right-hand edge of the carriageway or central reservation
- **Red** – marks the left-hand edge of the carriageway
- **Green** – separates slip roads from the motorway and indicates side roads or turn offs on carriageways
- **White** – separates the middle lanes on the motorway

It is also important not to forget about the other types of road and vehicle markings that you may come across, such as:

- Waiting restrictions
- Loading restrictions
- Zebra crossings
- School patrols
- Bus lanes
- Hazard warning plates

OXIDIZING AGENT

5.1

RADIOACTIVE

7

COMPRESSED GAS

2

PEDESTRIAN ZONE

Sat 10am - 7pm
Sun & Bank
Holidays
11am - 5pm

Mon - Fri
8.00 - 9.15 am
4.30 - 6.30 pm
Sat
8.00 - 9.15 am
12 noon - 1 pm

No loading
Mon - Fri
8.00 - 9.15 am
4.30 - 6.30 pm
Sat
8.00 - 9.15 am
12 noon - 1 pm

You should look at these more closely in your Highway Code book.

1. On a motorway reflective studs are inserted to indicate different road positions at night. In your folder copy out the key below and fill in the blanks to match the road stud colours (red, green, orange, white) with the correct road position.

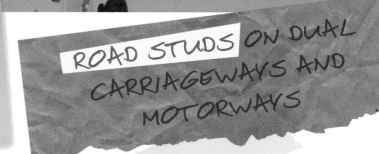

ROAD STUDS ON DUAL CARRIAGEWAYS AND MOTORWAYS

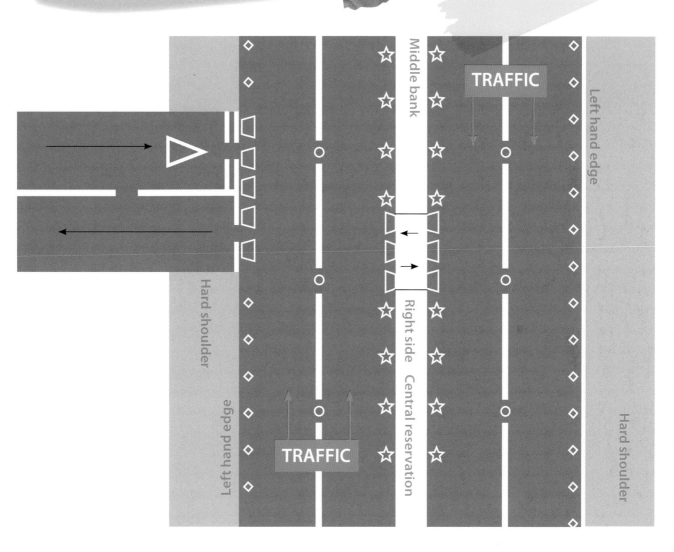

○ _____ studs separate the traffic lanes

◇ _____ studs mark the hard shoulder or left hand edge

▱ _____ studs mark a side or slip road

☆ _____ studs mark the right hand edge or central reservation

ROAD MARKINGS AND SIGNALS

FOR YOUR FOLDER

2. Use the *Highway Code* to help you write a description for each of the following road markings and signals in your folder.

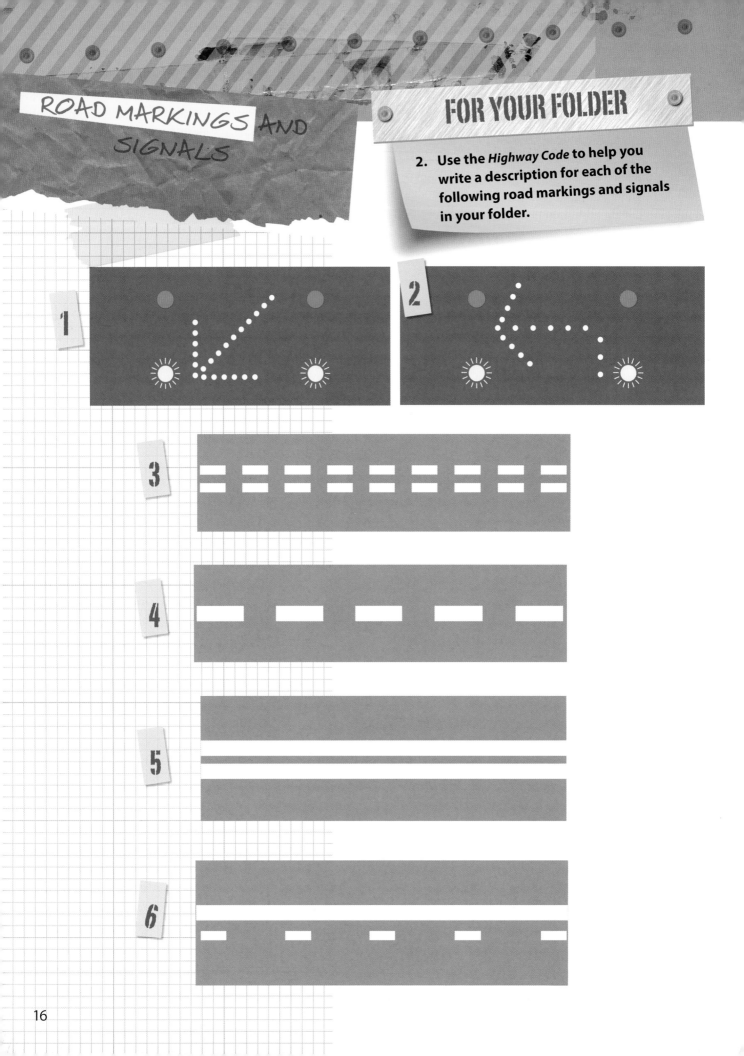

3. Use your *Highway Code* to help you name the hazard warnings below.

1

2

3

4

5

Left

Central

Right

4. What do double yellow lines beside a kerb mean?

5. What does a single yellow line beside a kerb mean?

6. What is the purpose of a bus lane?

Vehicle Manoeuvring

Highlighted below are some of the main manoeuvres you will have to make if driving a vehicle. It is important that you study each of these sections properly in your *Highway Code* book to fully inform yourself of the correct procedures.

ROAD JUNCTIONS

There are a number of different types of road junctions.

1. Road junctions
2. Box junctions
3. Traffic light controlled junctions

Road junctions inform you that you need to slow down or stop before entering another road. You need to take extra care at junctions, checking your position and speed when approaching them. Always make sure you check your mirrors and indicate in plenty of time before pulling out (mirror, signal, manoeuvre). Junctions are particularly dangerous for cyclists, motorcyclists and pedestrians, so watch out for them before you pull out or turn in.

Box junctions are a traffic controlled system set up to prevent traffic congestion at busy road junctions. These are usually identified as large, yellow boxes with criss-cross lines. Vehicles are not allowed to stop inside the box. These junctions are designed to allow motorists to move whenever their exit route is clear and to allow motorists to turn right safely.

Junctions controlled by traffic lights stop vehicles to allow pedestrians to cross roads safely. They also ease traffic congestion as each exit route is given a set amount of time to allow traffic through.

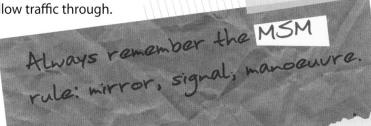

Always remember the MSM rule: mirror, signal, manoeuvre.

Roundabouts

When approaching a roundabout it is important to decide as early as possible which exit you need to take and get into the correct lane. You always give way to traffic on your right and should be especially aware of motorists that are already on the roundabout.

The blind spot

Blind spots are the parts of the road that you cannot see from the driving seat, even with use of your mirrors. Head rests in the back of a vehicle can impair a driver's vision when reversing and the door panels between the front and rear side windows can also obstruct a driver's vision when overtaking.

Reversing

Before reversing make sure there are no pedestrians, particularly children, or obstructions on the road behind you. Check your blind spot behind you. You should only reverse your vehicle for as long as is absolutely necessary.

Overtaking

You must keep in the left-hand lane unless you are overtaking. You overtake only on the right, unless traffic is moving in queues and the queue on your right is moving more slowly than you are. You must not use the hard shoulder to overtake.

To overtake you should drop back from the vehicle in front so that you can get a clear look at the road ahead. Take time to judge the speeds of any traffic on the road and take special care at night when visibility is poorer and distances are more difficult to judge. Check your mirrors, indicate in plenty of time, and then pull out (mirror, signal, manoeuvre). You need to double check before pulling out to overtake that no vehicles or motorcyclists are approaching quickly behind you. When you have pulled out accelerate past the slower moving vehicle. To pull back in you must again check your mirrors and indicate. Be sure not to pull back in too quickly as you may force the vehicle that you have passed to brake suddenly.

Road works

Special care is needed at road works. Watch out for and follow all the signs on the approach to and at the road works. They are often a cause of frustration for motorists and can lead to impatient manoeuvres. Where you know there are going to be road works you should allow more time for your journey to compensate for any delays.

Breakdowns

If you break down on the motorway, pull onto the hard shoulder. On any other road, if possible, remove your car from the road and put on your hazard lights to warn others of your presence.

FOR YOUR FOLDER

Look at the 'Roundabouts' section in your *Highway Code* book. Answer the following questions in relation to this section.

1. On reaching a roundabout, priority must be given to whom?

2. State two actions that a motorist needs to take on approach to a roundabout.

3. State two things that you must do before exiting a roundabout.

4. Why is it important to indicate at a roundabout?

5. Why is it important to be aware of motorists that are already on the roundabout?

FOR YOUR FOLDER

Look at the 'Overtaking' section in your *Highway Code* book. Answer the following questions in relation to this section.

1. On what side of the road do you overtake on?

2. If you see solid double white lines down the centre of a road, what do these mean?

3. Before overtaking what three checks should you make?

4. What three precautions must you take when overtaking large vehicles?

5. Name three instances where it may be unsafe to pass if you cannot see far enough ahead.

6. Why is it important not to cut in too quickly in front of another vehicle when overtaking?

CAUSES AND PREVENTION OF ROAD ACCIDENTS

There is a very good chance that you could be present at the scene of a road accident at some stage in your life. Statistics drawn up over the years have highlighted that drivers and passengers in vehicles have a 10% chance of being involved in an accident sometime within their life span. Every year the Police, DOE and Stormont Executive produce sets of statistics relating to road accidents in Northern Ireland. Statistics produced include the number of deaths on the roads, seat belt wearing rates and drink driving prosecutions. These figures are used to indicate problem areas that need to be addressed. The police may tackle target areas or publicity campaigns may follow to increase awareness of a deteriorating situation.

accident causes

We all use the roads as a means to get to wherever we need to go and no matter how we are travelling, whether in a vehicle or on foot, it should be done safely so that we do not risk our own lives or those of others. It is very important that you always concentrate fully on the road ahead, as a moment's lapse in concentration could be life threatening. Survivors of accidents who know they are responsible come up with all types of explanations and excuses. However, nine out of ten accidents are caused by some mistake or misjudgement by the driver or individual.

High risk areas

Adverse weather conditions

Physical and mental fitness of the driver

Vulnerable road users

Distractions

Speeding

The two most likely categories of drivers to have accidents are the young and elderly – those under the age of twenty-five and those who are over sixty-five. Among young drivers the main causes of road accidents are usually speeding or drinking and driving. Elderly people sometimes make misjudgements as a result of their failing eyesight and hearing. A few of the main accident causes are listed opposite:

All accidents are costly, not only because of damage expenses but also the even greater cost of death or serious injury. Unfortunately some families are forced to deal with unexpected and unnecessary deaths. Some people do survive road accidents but are left severely injured with limited quality of life, having to depend on others for support and survival. You probably know how difficult it is to watch some of the road safety advertisements on TV and hope that similar scenarios never happen to you.

High Risk Areas

On public roads there are a number of areas that have a high risk of road traffic accidents. You need to be very careful and aware of the possible dangers that can arise when approaching:

- **a bad bend** – You should slow down when approaching a bad bend because if you lose control of your vehicle you could end up on the other side of the road, which could cause a collision with oncoming traffic. Travelling at speed around a corner could also lead to your vehicle toppling or rolling over onto its side or roof.

- **a brow of a hill** – You should reduce your speed when approaching the brow of a hill because your forward vision will be restricted. You should anticipate possible hazards on the other side of the brow and be prepared to slow down or stop if required.

- **a hidden dip** – Dips in the road are often hidden. It is common to think you can see the entire road ahead and pull out to pass a slow moving vehicle. This is very dangerous because if you meet an oncoming vehicle you will be unprepared and could cause a head-on collision. You should only pull out to pass if the road ahead is straight and clear of traffic.

- **a residential area** – In residential areas there are often children playing in the street and sometimes dogs or cats running loose. Children and animals are not very aware of the dangers of the road and could run out in front of your vehicle. This could force you to brake or swerve suddenly, which could cause any traffic behind you to run into the back of your vehicle. If you are very unlucky you might even hit the child or animal, therefore it is important to drive slowly and alertly when travelling through residential areas. Parked cars are also a problem as a pedestrian crossing between them would not have a clear view of the road and could step out in front of your passing vehicle. Similarly, someone opening a car door without checking the traffic could cause an accident, as you would have to brake or swerve suddenly to avoid the door. If you are parked along

a residential area...

the side of a road you should always check your mirrors for approaching traffic before getting out of your vehicle.

Certain times of the day may increase the risk of accidents because of increased vehicle and pedestrian activity, such as the following:

School/Religious/Bank holidays

7-9 am	people going to work and school
3-4 pm	schools closing
5-6 pm	people going home from work

Schools in particular can add to congestion, with buses and parents leaving their children to or collecting them from school. School opening and closing times will also increase pedestrian movement. If driving at these times you need to be vigilant, as school children may dash across a road to catch up with friends or to catch their bus. The start and end of a working day will also increase traffic congestion. Between the working hours of 8 am and 6 pm there may be an increase of vans and lorries on the roads doing deliveries. Holiday periods will also increase traffic on the roads, especially in good weather, because people will want to take trips with their families or get some shopping done, to make the most of their free time. This may lead to congestion in specific places such as good shopping towns, country parks or seaside resorts.

Adverse Weather Conditions

Weather hazards cause many problems for drivers. You must be aware of the different ways in which each weather condition can affect your driving manoeuvres and the road conditions. You should then be able to drive safely and cope with any problems that are presented to you. Pedestrians are also affected by changes in weather conditions. Weather hazards such as fog, snow, ice, wind and rain are the main problems as they affect hearing, vision and balance. Driving at night also has its problems.

Equipment

It is important that both pedestrians and cyclists make themselves as visible as possible on the roads, especially in poor conditions. Bright, fluorescent or reflective clothing should be worn on some part of the body so that they stand out when the lights of a passing vehicle shine on them.

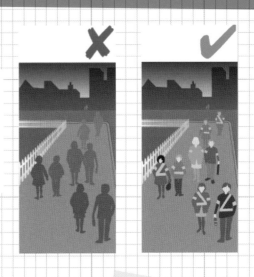

Fluorescent materials work better in daylight because they react to sunlight's ultra violet rays, causing fluorescent glare and making it stand out against its background. Fluorescent materials come in orange, yellow or lime green colours. At night or when visibility is poor, fluorescent materials are less noticeable and therefore reflective materials are used instead. Reflective materials work best at night and reflect the light produced by vehicle headlights straight back at the driver. Thousands of tiny, shiny beads in the material act in a similar way to the white cats eyes on the road, its reflective properties shining or reflecting the light straight back at the driver. Clothing is available that combines both fluorescent and reflective properties. Pedestrians, cyclists, motorcyclists and horse riders should use a range of reflective aids to make them more noticeable on the roads, such as reflectors on bicycles, reflective stickers, reflective and fluorescent armbands, hats, helmets and other items of clothing.

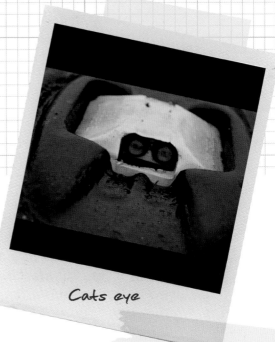

Cats eye

Cold weather equipment

During the winter months additional emergency equipment should be carried in a car. Some of this equipment is listed opposite:

First aid kit (bandages)
De-icer spray
Jump leads
Torch
Reflective Jacket
Mobile Phone

Rain

The main problem for road users in the rain is poor visibility. Heavy rain and spray from other vehicles can be constant and difficult to clear quickly with windscreen wipers. Wet roads require increased braking distances and tyres have less grip because water makes the road surface greasy and slippery. To drive safely you should drive slowly, with dipped headlights, making sure that your windows are clear and not misted over. By driving slowly the vehicle will have more grip on the road as the tyre treads will be able to remove a greater amount of surface water faster. As tyre treads are needed to disperse the water and keep grip with the road surface, badly worn tyres can also cause road traffic accidents in wet conditions due to the reduced tread depth. Similarly, driving too fast will not allow the treads the opportunity to disperse enough water, leading to reduced grip. You must also remember that when driving in wet conditions braking and stopping distances will be at least doubled as a result of the reduced tyre grip. The brakes will not be as effective as they would be in dry conditions because they will be wet and need drying out. Brake pads that are wet are more likely to allow the discs and drums to continue slipping instead of grinding them to a halt. To compensate for these conditions you need to drive much slower, apply the brakes gently and allow time for your vehicle to stop.

Pedestrians may be more difficult to see in wet conditions and should ideally wear fluorescent or reflective clothing. Wet clothing is generally dull and harder for motorists to see, as well as being heavy and affecting pedestrians' speed. Rain drowns out noise, making it more difficult to hear oncoming traffic and pedestrians may tend to cross roads in a hurry to get out of the rain. Remember hoods and umbrellas keep you dry but reduce hearing and visibility. When driving you must thus be very aware of pedestrians walking alongside or crossing roads, as their hearing and visibility may be impaired, and they may be more inclined to lose their balance as surfaces can be very slippery under foot.

Aquaplaning

Tyre treads are used to remove rain and surface water to increase tyre grip with the road surface. Driving at a high speed makes it more difficult to remove a large volume of rain and surface water. Therefore a vehicle's grip on the road may be greatly reduced, causing the wheels to lift up off the road onto the top of the surface water. This in turn causes brakes and steering to be less effective and will be improved only if the vehicle's speed is reduced.

Flooded roads

If you have to drive through very deep water you should drive carefully but not too slowly as this may result in your engine stalling and it could prove difficult to re-start. However, if you drive too quickly you may get water in the engine or the electrics, which could lead to very serious and expensive damage. After driving through deep water you should test your brakes. If they have water on them they may need drying out. You are most likely to drive into a flood at night when visibility is poor. You should never drive through water that is more than 250 mm deep. The safest option is always to try and find an alternative route.

Sun

We all enjoy the good weather and sunny conditions. However, the sun's brightness can blind road users and impair their driving. Similarly, sun shining after a shower of rain can reflect off the wet road causing poor visibility. Silver vehicles in particular are harder to see when the sun is shining. Sun that is blocked from reaching the road surface can form deep shadows, causing dullness, and a pedestrian walking along the side of the road in this deep shadow may be difficult for motorists to see.

You should wear sunglasses and use your sun visor to improve your vision and block out the sun's glare when driving. In winter the sun is lower in the sky and sun visors do not provide as much protection as they would in the summer months. If you have to drive a long distance in warm weather it is important to keep your vehicle well ventilated by either winding the window down or turning on the air conditioning. This will help prevent you from becoming drowsy.

Driving at night

Dawn and dusk are the two most difficult times to drive, when it is neither bright nor dark. It is easier to see vehicles in the light of day and on a clear dark night when lights are clearly visible. Before setting out on a journey, you should make sure that all your lights, both front and rear, are in full working order. This is one of the checks carried out during the MOT. It is used to see if a vehicle's lights are focused and aligned properly, to ensure the clearest and brightest vision of the road ahead. One problem with driving at night is the blinding lights of approaching and passing vehicles. If driving a long distance, these conditions can be extremely tiring on the eyes, especially for older motorists. Therefore it is important that you are considerate and dip you headlights when approaching or following other vehicles because the brightness of a full beam can be blinding. The full beam should be used *only* when the road ahead is clear. Motorists often use their headlights to 'flash' at other vehicles to indicate some form of a warning, for example, if the road ahead has animals running loose on it.

Another common hazard for motorists in the dark is how poor light makes judging the speed and distance of other vehicles more difficult. It is therefore very important to take extra care, especially when pulling out of a side road or junction. You should be particularly aware of lighting up times. The 'Lighting requirements' section in the *Highway Code* clearly states that vehicle lights must be switched on half an hour after sunset and half an hour before sunrise. What you have to remember is that where there are no street lights, vision will be restricted to the range of your vehicle's headlights. Therefore vehicle speed must be reduced to compensate for the lack of forward vision. Parking at night is another major problem for motorists and is addressed in detail in the 'Parking at night' section in your *Highway Code* book. You should take a few minutes to read these laws in greater detail.

Fog

Fog causes poor visibility for all types of road user. When driving in fog you should always drive slowly, using dipped headlights, along with front and rear fog lights. Fog lights are very strong and can blind other motorists if used in dry or clear conditions, therefore they must only be used when visibility is poor. Fog comes and goes, it can be thick in one place and thin in another, and can therefore catch road users off guard. On a straight part of the road visibility could be very good and suddenly, around the next corner, visibility could be very poor as a result of scattered fog. Fog can affect a road user's sight and hearing. This makes it not only harder to see other vehicles but also to judge their speed and distance. When pulling out of a side road or junction in fog, you should wind down the window because listening for vehicles can sometimes be easier than seeing them. Sometimes you may even need to sound your horn to make others aware of your presence. Similarly to in wet conditions, pedestrians may be more difficult to see and their hearing may be impaired in the fog. Fluorescent or reflective clothing will make them more visible to motorists but it is essential that they take more time to look and listen for traffic when crossing the road.

Adverse weather conditions summarised

Condition	Effects on driver	What should you do?
RAIN	• Reduces visibility and increases braking distances. • Tyres have less grip. • Pedestrians wear hoods and umbrellas in the rain. This decreases their vision and hearing, which may result in them walking out in front of a car. • Roads become very slippy.	• The slower you drive the more grip you have. • Use dipped headlights. • Clear condensation off the windows using the demister and headed screen element. • Wear reflective clothing.
AQUAPLANING	• This is when the tyres rise up off the road onto the top of surface water caused by heavy rain. • Causes the steering and brakes to become ineffective, making the driver lose control of the vehicle.	• Reduce speed immediately.
FLOODED ROADS	• More likely to drive into a flood at night when visibility is poor. • If driving too fast your car might come to a violent stop allowing water to damage the engine. If driving too slowly your vehicle may stall and be difficult to restart. • Brakes become wet and ineffective.	• Do not drive through water that is more than 250 mm deep. • Drive slowly through shallow floods so that the electrics in the engine do not get damaged.
SUN	• Blinds road users. • Reduces visibility. • Sun reflects off wet roads. • Warm weather can make a driver drowsy. • Sun that is blocked from the road can create dullness and deep shadows.	• Wear tinted sunglasses and use sun visors. • Keep vehicles well ventilated.
DRIVING AT NIGHT	• Lights of other road users can be blinding. • Difficult to judge the speed and distance of other vehicles. • Where there is no street lighting your vision is restricted to the range of your headlights.	• Drive at a slower speed. • Dipped headlights should be used at dusk. • Dipped headlights should be used when approaching other vehicles. • Check all lights before setting off on a journey.
FOG	• Reduces visibility not only for you but for everyone. • It also drowns out noise. • Vehicles with no rear fog lights and vehicles parked along the side of roads can be difficult to see. • It is hard to judge the speed and distance of other vehicles.	• Always use dipped headlights and fog lights both front and back. • Drive slowly. • When turning out of a road open the window and listen out for approaching vehicles. • Sometimes you may need to sound the horn. • Follow the fog code.

ICE	• Roads can become slippy and the car becomes harder to control. • Braking and stopping distances can be increased. • Black ice (surface water which freezes on the top of the road) is difficult to see and is often mistaken for a wet patch, catching many drivers unawares.	• Check the road for ice before starting out on a journey. • Look out for sparkling reflections which indicate frost. • Reduce speed and allow more time for your journey. • Drive slowly and avoid heavy braking.
SNOW	• Causes roads to become slippy. • Reduces visibility as it builds up on the window screen and headlights. • Wheel arches can be blocked restricting wheel movement. • Can grind all movement to a halt. • Vehicle handling and steering can become more difficult because roads are slippy. • Braking and stopping distances can be increased.	• Use dipped headlights in falling snow. • Drive and manoeuvre slowly, staying well back from the vehicle in front. • Going up and down hills should be done in a low gear. • Clear windscreens, lights and wheel arches before setting off.
STRONG WINDS	• Rubbish blowing in towns distracts drivers' attention. • In the country falling branches and trees can be a problem. • On open roads, motorways and bridges, crosswinds can affect the handling of a vehicle. • Headwinds restrict and slow the movement of cyclists and pedestrians.	• Reduce speeds so that you can comfortably cope with the steering of the vehicle. • Be wary of passing high-sided vehicles as they could sway into your path.

FOR YOUR FOLDER

1. Why is fog considered to be a major cause of motorway accidents?
2. How does fog affect a driver?
3. Make a list of procedures you should follow in foggy conditions.
4. Why is it important to keep a vehicle well ventilated in the warm weather?
5. How does the sun affect a driver's sight?
6. Why is the sun a greater hazard in winter?
7. State two reasons why it is important for motorists to reduce their speed in wet weather.
8. How can motorists make themselves more visible on the roads?
9. Why are pedestrians vulnerable in wet conditions?
10. List four things a motorist can do to improve his or her own safety when driving in snow.

FOR YOUR FOLDER

1. What is black ice?
2. State two things a driver could do to reduce the risk of an accident in icy conditions.
3. What does the term aquaplaning mean?
4. How is a motorist affected by aquaplaning?
5. Name two precautions a driver should take when approaching a flood.
6. Where are strong winds most dangerous to motorists?
7. Why are high-sided vehicles vulnerable in strong winds?
8. How do strong winds affect a motorist in a town or city?
9. Why is it important to dip your headlights when approaching other vehicles?
10. Make a list of equipment needed in cold weather.

Alcohol

People drink for various different reasons. It may be to celebrate a special occasion, to be sociable, or even to release stress or worry. Many of the effects of drinking alcohol that make people feel relaxed and happy can also impair their driving skills. Your chances of having a road accident are much higher when under the influence of alcohol because drinking alcohol affects your body in the following ways:

- You cannot coordinate and control your muscles as well as you can normally because alcohol is a depressant.
- It takes you longer to react, so it is more difficult to deal with the unexpected.
- It impairs your decision-making process.
- You are less able to judge speed and distance.
- You are often more daring and reckless, making you more likely to drive fast.

Alcohol is broken down and dispersed by the liver, and eating before and after drinking only slows down this process. There is no fast way to remove alcohol from the bloodstream.

What people sometimes forget is that all drinks have different strengths, that will affect them in different ways and at different speeds. Many people think that it is safe and legal to have one drink and drive. It is not that simple. Different measures of drink contain different amounts of alcohol. The current level for a drink drive prosecution is 35 micrograms of alcohol per 100 millilitres of breath.

KEY POINTS – LEGAL LIMITS

35 micrograms of alcohol per 100 millilitres of breath

80 milligrams of alcohol per 100 millilitres of blood

107 milligrams of alcohol per 100 millilitres of urine

There are two laws regarding drink driving:

BEING OVER THE LIMIT

DRIVING UNDER THE INFLUENCE

Driving after any intake of alcohol leaves you open to prosecution. This is usually a hefty fine and disqualification. The simplest rule to follow is:

IF YOU DRIVE, DON'T DRINK, IF YOU DRINK, DON'T DRIVE.

Drugs

Unfortunately in our society today there is an increasing demand for drugs. When drugs are mentioned, generally people think of illegal drugs, such as cocaine, ecstasy, heroine and marijuana. What they do not realise is that drugs prescribed by hospitals, doctors and chemists, such as pain killers, tranquillisers and sleeping pills, can also have side effects that can affect their judgement and reactions. Therefore if taking any sort of a medication you must make sure you read the instructions on the box or bottle before taking a vehicle out onto the roads. You must remember that you will be putting yourself and other motorists at risk if you decide to drive under the influence of drugs. Therefore the police and courts will not be sympathetic if you are caught under this influence and will usually impose a large fine, penalty points or driving licence disqualification.

FOR YOUR FOLDER

1. State three ways that alcohol affects the body.
2. Why do different drinks affect the body in different ways?
3. Is alcohol a stimulant or a depressant?
4. How is alcohol dispersed from the blood stream?
5. Why should people not drink and drive?
6. What are the three legal limits for drinking and driving?
7. What could happen to a driver found over the legal limit?

Fatigue (tiredness)

When you are tired your reactions are slower and less effective. A number of factors can cause you to become tired. A few of these are listed below:

- Distance (in the length of journey)
- Warm weather
- Boredom of traffic delays
- Monotony of motorway driving

It is very important that you keep the vehicle well ventilated and stop often to refresh yourself when travelling long distances, as this should help reduce the effects of tiredness. If travelling by car with another adult who is insured on the vehicle it is a good idea to share the driving. Using a route planner prior to setting off allows you to plan your journey, which should help you arrive at your destination as quickly and hopefully as stress-free as possible.

THINK

1. Take a look at this week's local papers for incidents where people have been prosecuted for drink driving.
2. Look at the penalty points table in your *Highway Code* book.
   List the two drinking and driving offences and the main differences between their penalties.

Vision

As you get older your eyesight may let you down. Unless you take the time to visit the opticians, it will only be tested once in your driving life – when taking your first driving test. During your first driving test the vehicle test examiner will ask and expect you to be able to read a vehicle registration plate from a distance of 20.5 metres.

As you age your vision can be affected in two main ways:

1. **Peripheral vision** relates to your side vision. This refers to your ability to see objects and movements that could become a hazard outside of your direct line of vision. For example, if a small child was running across an open area, heading for the road, a motorist with limited peripheral vision may not see the child in time to react quickly.

2. **Tunnel vision** is an extremely restricted visual field, which can result in a narrow, circular vision that focuses only on one spot on the road. This usually occurs in middle aged or older age groups.

Colour blindness is also a common problem for many motorists, especially in determining the colour of traffic lights because certain colours, such as greens, browns, and reds, are deemed the hardest to recognise.

It is very important that you visit the opticians if you suspect that your eyesight is deteriorating because you may need a pair of prescribed glasses. If you wear glasses or lenses you must only wear them in the conditions they are prescribed for, as they could also restrict or affect your vision if worn at any other time. If your vision seems more limited on bright days or at night you might find it helpful to wear tinted glasses or pull down your sun visor to block out sunlight and headlight glare.

Stress and depression

Driving while stressed or upset can affect your concentration, as your mind is not likely to be on your driving. You are more likely to make careless manoeuvres or mistakes if you are distracted, putting yourself and others at risk. Stress can make you impatient, increase aggression towards other motorists and affect your judgement. Running late, exam pressure, a busy day at work or reliving an argument are all likely to affect your focus and impair your reactions. For example, if you are stuck behind an elderly driver on a bad country road you may decide to risk overtaking if you are in a hurry.

Vulnerable road users

When driving on the roads you must always show consideration towards all other road users and pedestrians. Some people will be more vulnerable on the roads than others. The young, the elderly, the disabled and non-motorised road users are all more vulnerable on the road than vehicle drivers who are fit and able.

Age

As people get older their eyesight and hearing sometimes deteriorates, which can slow their reactions and impair their driving. Poor eyesight can lead to inaccurate manoeuvres, which could cause an accident. As a driver you should be patient with older drivers and give them as much time and room as possible – they have as much right to use the road as younger drivers.

Young children are not fully aware of the dangers associated with the road. When walking, adults should always keep children to the inside of the road or footpath in case they walk out in front of a vehicle. When driving, you should always reduce your speed if you see children playing nearby or walking on the road because their actions can be unpredictable. Similarly, you should slow down if you see a person with a pram, as the pram's extra width and length makes it more vulnerable. Someone may even try to cross between parked cars, pushing the pram slightly out onto the road to get a good view. People with prams should ideally cross at a designated crossing point, such as a zebra or light controlled crossing. However, if there is not crossing point nearby they should find an open space to cross, where they can clearly see the road in both directions and any traffic behind them.

Disability

Wheel chair users are limited by their chair's speed and movement when crossing the road. They will not be able to react as quickly as pedestrians on foot. Their chairs can also reduce their visibility, as they are quite low down, sometimes making crossing between parked cars dangerous. Similarly, people with leg or foot injuries will have similar speed and reaction problems, as they are limited by their walking aids. As a driver you must therefore look out, slow down and stop for people with mobility problems crossing the road.

Disabled drivers can find certain manoeuvres difficult in their vehicles, such as parking, changing gears or even getting out of their vehicle. As a driver you must be aware and considerate of disabled drivers to prevent accidents occurring. Some vehicles are specifically designed for disabled drivers and these are known as mobility vehicles. Alterations may include a hand only operated braking system, button controls, a swivel seat to enable easy access and a dashboard lever operated gear stick.

People who are blind or partially sighted generally rely on sound, guide dogs or other people for assistance. This can make crossing the road quite difficult therefore you should always show consideration by slowing down and stopping to allow plenty of time for them to cross.

1. Why are young children vulnerable on the roads?
2. How should a person with a pram cross a road were there are parked cars?
3. List two things that might affect an elderly person's driving skills.
4. If you see a blind or partially sighted person crossing a road when you are driving what should you do?

Cycling

Cycling on the roads today requires your full attention and above all, awareness of other road users. Cyclists can be regarded as vulnerable road users because a safety framework, like that of vehicles, does not surround them. Therefore if you are cycling you must be aware of the movements of all the vehicles around you. It is also important that you carry out your manoeuvres safely and signal correctly to inform other motorists of your intentions. Weather conditions can also prove problematic to cyclists. Rain will leave the roads greasy and slippy, and strong winds or large vehicles passing at speed can cause a loss of balance. Children are especially at risk when riding a bicycle because they generally have less knowledge and experience of the road and its procedures than an adult.

It is essential that all cyclists wear the appropriate safety clothing and the three most important items are:

CYCLE HELMET

PADDED CLOTHING

FLUORESCENT CLOTHING

It is important to avoid wearing long coats and loose clothing when cycling because these could become tangled in the bicycle chain. Children age ten and above can take part in the National Cycling Proficiency Scheme (NCPS), which provides safety training in cycle riding. This scheme enables the young cyclist to gain knowledge and understanding of how to cycle safely on the roads.

In Northern Ireland all bicycles used on public roads are expected to have a white front light, a red rear light and a red rear reflector. Before taking a bicycle onto the roads you must make sure that your bicycle meets the following legal requirements:

LIGHTS AND REFLECTORS ARE CLEAN AND IN GOOD WORKING ORDER

TYRES ARE IN GOOD CONDITION AND AT THE CORRECT PRESSURE

BRAKES AND GEARS ARE WORKING CORRECTLY

Distractions for motorists

Road accidents can occur very suddenly. A lack of concentration by a driver, rider or pedestrian may unfortunately lead to death or serious injury. You must learn to ignore everyday distractions when driving to enable you to concentrate fully on your driving and the road ahead.

Internal distractions

You must be aware of and avoid creating internal distractions before setting out on a journey. A number of distractions inside the vehicle that you may have to contend with are listed below:

- Fumbling with radio controls and not concentrating on the road ahead could force you to brake suddenly, sway or manoeuvre carelessly.

- Pets that are not properly secured, out of sight, could distract your attention and lead to careless driving.

- Children or objects that are not properly secured can also distract you if they are moving around inside the vehicle, are shouting or asking you questions.

- Attempting to read a map while driving could be very dangerous because you would not be concentrating on the road ahead.

- Using a mobile phone while driving leaves you only one hand free to drive with, reducing your control of the vehicle. Your concentration will also be on your conversation and not on the road in front of you.

- Trying to eat and drink while driving again leaves you only one hand free to drive with, reducing your control.

Any of these actions could lead to an unfortunate accident and some are even illegal.

Distractions for Motorists....

External distractions

In towns and cities there will be more external distractions that can impair your concentration when driving. A number of distractions outside the vehicle that you may have to contend with are listed below:

- Children playing along the side of a road or a ball bouncing in front of your vehicle will obviously distract your attention from the road ahead, which could force you to brake suddenly, swerve or manoeuvre carelessly.

- Pedestrians may walk out in front of your vehicle and you may have to brake or swerve suddenly.

- Dogs or animals on the loose may run out in front of your vehicle, again forcing you to brake or swerve.

- Advertisements on billboards may take a moment to read and divert your concentration from the road ahead. This could prevent you from braking in time if another vehicle in front of you slows down. You may also be slow to move off from a junction if you do not notice that the lights have changed, irritating other road users.

- Litter blowing may catch your eye and distract your attention from the road ahead.

- Other motorists' manoeuvres may distract you or cause you to hesitate as you try to figure out their intentions.

- Road accidents can distract your attention from the road ahead as you look to see if there are any casualties or damages. Try to concentrate on the road in front of you in case you cause another accident.

 **THINK**

Think about the different forms of advertising on the roads. Explain how such advertising can distract drivers and the possible consequences of this distraction.

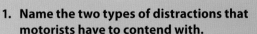 **FOR YOUR FOLDER**

1. **Name the two types of distractions that motorists have to contend with.**
2. **Make a list of some distractions inside a vehicle.**
3. **Make a list of some distractions outside a vehicle.**
4. **What consequences could there be for a motorist because of these distractions?**
5. **Explain why using a mobile phone while driving is dangerous for a motorist.**
6. **Why are road accidents a distraction to motorists?**

Speeding

Speeding is one of the most frequent causes of road accidents. Disregarding speed limits is more common among drivers under 25 years old than drivers over 25. Young drivers, often males, can be too confident and some take risks. As they are generally less experienced than older drivers, they often do not realise the dangers associated with speed and increased stopping distances, particularly in the ever-changing road conditions. The government has introduced a number of measures to attempt to reduce such accidents. For example, warning signs inform motorists of the dangers on the road ahead. Traffic calming measures, such as those listed below, are also used to slow down the speed of motorists in residential or urban areas:

SPEED CUSHIONS
SPEED HUMPS
ROAD NARROWING
HORIZONTAL DEFLECTION
GATEWAYS

Penalty points can be issued if speed limits are not adhered to on public roads. Speed cameras have also been introduced within the last ten years to assist the police traffic branch in catching and penalising speeding motorists. These cameras can be permanent or temporary. Each type of road has a national speed limit that must be adhered to by motorists.

Speed Limits	Built-up areas*	Single carriage-ways	Dual carriage-ways	Motorways
Type of vehicle	mph (km/h)	mph (km/h)	mph (km/h)	mph (km/h)
Cars & motorcycles (including car-derived vans up to 2 tonnes maximum laden weight)	30 (48)	60 (96)	70 (112)	70 (112)
Cars towing caravans or trailers (including car-derived vans and motorcycles)	30 (48)	50 (80)	60 (96)	60 (96)
Buses, coaches and minibuses (not exceeding 12 metres in overall length)	30 (48)	50 (80)	60 (96)	70 (112)
Goods vehicles (not exceeding 7.5 tonnes maximum laden weight)	30 (48)	50 (80)	60 (96)	70 (112)
Goods vehicles (exceeding 7.5 tonnes maximum laden weight)	30 (48)	40 (64)	50 (80)	60 (96)

Enforcement (The Law)

There are a large number of road traffic laws that control the operation of motor vehicles. The most important of these laws are summarised in the *Highway Code* book, which provides information on all the correct road procedures. These laws address issues such as driving on the roads, drinking and driving, the use of both front and rear seat belts and parking restrictions. The police, DVA Enforcement Officers, Parking Attendants, and Customs and Excise Officers are mainly responsible for enforcing these laws. DVA Enforcement Officers concentrate on dealing with motorists that have no road tax. Parking Attendants are employed in towns and cities to issue parking tickets to vehicles parked in no parking zones or double parked on a road. They also check that vehicles parked in proper parking zones have paid the correct tariff for the waiting times. Customs and Excise Officers specialise in checking vehicles for the illegal use of fuel. For example, diesel vehicles are legally required to use white diesel, however, some motorists will buy the cheaper, red, agricultural diesel and hope that they will not be checked by customs.

Most police forces have a traffic division which specialise in road traffic offences, such as speeding and drink driving. In Northern Ireland there is a penalty points system in place whereby if a motorist receives twelve penalty points for traffic offences within a three year period, the driver will automatically lose his or her license and be disqualified for a set period of time imposed by the courts. Remember that after passing your driving test, as a restricted driver you will have to re-sit your test if you receive six penalty points within your first two years driving. Speeding, badly worn tyres,

no seat belt, drink driving and careless driving are just some of the offences that will lead to a driver picking up penalty points. There are two types of offences:

ENDORSABLE TICKETS
- carry a fine and penalty points

NON-ENDORSABLE TICKETS
- just carry a fine

Education

All road users have a responsibility to be aware of the safe and proper way to use the roads. Education starts in the home, where our parents constantly remind us about the dangers involved with using the roads. In primary schools this knowledge is reinforced by learning the **Green Cross Code**. Two important points highlighted in the green cross code are:

1. Stop, Look and Listen
2. Cross from a safe place

Some primary schools also introduce their pupils to the National Cycling Proficiency Scheme (NCPS), usually in primary six or seven. This scheme teaches children how to cycle safely on the roads and makes them aware of possible dangers. Some Secondary, Grammar, Comprehensive and High schools offer Motor Vehicle and Road User Studies (MVRUS) as a GCSE subject for one or two years at age fifteen and above. This course enables the pupils to learn about all road laws, vehicle manoeuvres and traffic management as well as an element of practical moped riding. In a final attempt to educate all road users, at age 17 a computerised theory element based on the *Highway Code* book must be passed before taking the practical driving test. To ensure your own safety and the safety of others on the roads it is best to take driving lessons with a specialist instructor. By doing so you will learn all the correct procedures and manoeuvres properly and have the best possible chance of passing the practical driving test.

Educational Timeline

- Education starts in the home by our parents at an early age

- Primary schools teach the Green Cross Code and NCPS

- At years 11 and 12 a GCSE in MVRUS can be taught

- At 17 years old a computerised theory test must be passed before taking the driving test

- The **Department of the Environment (DOE)** continues to promote and educate road safety through various advertising campaigns

- The DOE Road Safety Branch have launched a web site www.roadsafetyni.gov.uk. This web site is a useful teaching and learning tool for promoting road safety. It is set up with four main areas:

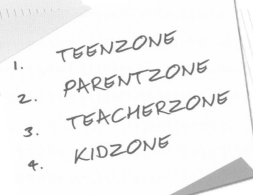

1. TEENZONE
2. PARENTZONE
3. TEACHERZONE
4. KIDZONE

A number of publicity campaigns have been set up over the years to make the general public aware of the dangers of using public roads. Anti-drink-driving campaigns are probably the most publicised, especially in the lead up to the Christmas period. The consequences of speeding and not wearing your seat belt are often well documented in local papers and adverts are often played on the radio, TV and posted on billboards. 'Be safe, be seen' is a campaign used to highlight the dangers of children coming home from school in the dark winter evenings. Reflective and fluorescent clothing and equipment has also been distributed to pupils in many schools.

FOR YOUR FOLDER

1. **What are the three main approaches to accident prevention?**

2. **What two main areas is engineering split up into?**

3. **What does traffic engineering involve?**

4. **What does vehicle engineering involve?**

5. **What are the two main areas of vehicle engineering?**

6. **What aspects of a vehicle does primary safety look at?**

7. **What aspects of a vehicle does secondary safety look at?**

8. **What is enforcement?**

9. **Make a list of the different ways in which you can be educated in road safety.**

THINK

Choose one of the following advertising campaigns and research its aims and success on the Internet:

- Speeding (DOE)
- Seat belts (DOE)
- Drinking And Driving (DOE)
- Be Safe, Be Seen (District Policing Board)
- Watch out For Motorcyclists (DOE)
- Stop, Look, Listen, Live (DOE)

Seat belts

Wearing seat belts saves lives and reduces the risk of serious injury in an accident. The seat belt is an essential secondary safety item fitted inside vehicles and should always be put on before setting out on a journey. Seat belts are discussed in more detail in Chapter 2, on page 55.

Chapter Two

LEGAL REQUIREMENTS

MOTOR INSURANCE

Any motorist taking a vehicle out onto the roads must be insured to drive it. Motor insurance will provide you with financial protection if you are involved in an accident on the roads.

Types of insurance

There are different types of insurance cover and the following terminology is used to explain the various types of cover available:

First party/policy holder/proposer	This is any motorist with or looking for insurance.
Second party/broker	This is the insurance company or insurance company's representative selling the insurance.
Third party	This is any other person that becomes involved in a road accident.
Premium	The price paid for insurance.
Policy	All the details of your insurance cover and the factors used to determine your premium.
Certificate	Legal proof of insurance.

Types of insurance...

Cover note	This is a temporary insurance certificate covering the driver for 30–60 days while a permanent hardcopy of the certificate is being drawn up.
Proposal form	A question form that the applicant fills in to outline the facts needed for the contract.
Underwriter	The person within the insurance company who is responsible for deciding whether or not to accept an insurance proposal based on the information provided by the road user.
Utmost good faith	Describes an individual that acted honestly with regard to an insurance claim.
Declined task/risk	An insurance company may not pay a claim if the road user has not honestly informed them of any important issues, such as the road user has a driving conviction. When seeking insurance the applicant is often asked if he or she has ever been declined before.
Indemnity	Compensation for loss or damage, restoring a person's financial position to what it was before the loss occurred.
Renewal notice	A reminder that your insurance for the year or six months is coming to an end, the details of the new start date and the amount to be paid for the following period.
Excess	This is the amount that you, as the owner, must pay for the damages if you have an accident and are at fault. Usually a fixed sum or percentage, this amount will be agreed by both the insurance company and yourself when the policy is being drawn up. The insurance company pays the remaining damage costs.
No claims bonus	Each year your insurance premium will be reduced if you do not claim from the insurance company. The percentage discount rises each year. After five years the premium will not be reduced any further but remain at its lower price.
Protected bonus	This protects your no claims bonus. It will cost more to add this agreement to a policy.
Knock for knock	This is where an insurance company will only cover the damage costs to the vehicle they insure, regardless of who is at fault.
Green card	Not applicable in Europe after the introduction of the EU. However, it may still be necessary for those driving outside of the EU.
Agent	Businesses looking to sell motor insurance.
Personal liability	Accepting responsibility for causing a road accident and what you are personally responsible for paying.

There are three types of motor insurance:

1. Third party

This is a basic type of motor insurance that covers you if you damage the property of or injure a third party while you are driving. However, it does not cover you for any damage you cause to yourself or your vehicle.

2. Third party fire and theft

This type of insurance is exactly the same as third party, with the additional benefit that it also allows you to claim if your car is stolen or set on fire.

3. Fully comprehensive

This type of insurance covers all parties involved in an accident. It is the most expensive type of insurance because it provides the best protection. If you have comprehensive insurance you are also covered to drive another person's car, but only third party. If you are involved in an accident while driving someone else's vehicle you will have to pay for any damages caused to that vehicle. You can add an 'any driver clause' to your vehicle, guaranteeing that anyone with a valid driving licence is insured to drive your car. However, this will obviously cost more.

If you are considering driving someone else's vehicle on the road it is a good idea to check what you will be covered for with your insurance company.

FOR YOUR FOLDER

1. What does the term policy holder mean?

2. What does the term no claims bonus mean?

3. What is the difference between an insurance policy and an insurance certificate?

Factors affecting the cost of motor insurance

There are a number of factors that affect the cost of motor insurance.

The driver

- Gender
- Age
- Driving record (any previous claims, convictions or penalty points)
- Occupation
- Residence

The vehicle

- Type and size
- Security (alarm)
- Parking location
- Type of insurance cover
- Other named drivers (especially those under 21 or over 65)

When applying for insurance you will be asked various questions about these factors, allowing the insurance company to measure your level of risk. The company can then calculate the cost of insurance and provide a quote for either six months or one year. It is essential that you answer these questions honestly because if you provide the company with any false information they do not have to pay your claim if you are involved in an accident. It is in your best interests to try and truthfully convince insurance companies that you are a low risk driver. The lower your risk, the less you will have to pay for insurance.

The age of a driver greatly influences insurance premiums. Young male drivers, aged between 17 and 24, will usually have to pay a high premium because insurance companies see them as the highest risk category. They are thought to be risk-takers, who drive too fast in cars that are too powerful for them to handle. Elderly drivers may also have to pay high insurance premiums because they are also considered to be high risk candidates. This is because some elderly drivers have failing health, eyesight and hearing. Insurance companies believe this can slow their reactions and make them more likely to misjudge distances.

The road user's driving record is a crucial factor in determining an insurance premium. A 'no claims bonus' is a valuable asset. Each year your insurance premium will be reduced if you do not claim from the insurance company. It can decrease your premium by as much as 70% in your sixth year without claiming. After your sixth year it will not be reduced any further. A rough guide to the yearly discount is summarised in the table below:

Year	Percentage discount
1	30%
2	40%
3	50%
4	60%
5	65%
5 years + and over 50 years old	70%

FOR YOUR FOLDER

1. **List the main factors that influence the cost of insurance.**
2. **Why is a driver's age an important factor in calculating the cost of insurance?**
3. **List the three main types of insurance.**
4. **Briefly explain what third party insurance covers.**

FOR YOUR FOLDER

5. **What type of insurance is the most expensive?**
6. **What is the purpose of a cover note?**
7. **What does the term 'indemnity' mean?**
8. **What does the term 'any driver clause' mean?**

LEGAL DOCUMENTATION

All the details of your insurance cover and the factors used to determine your premium will be displayed and documented in your insurance policy. However, your most important document is your insurance certificate. This provides a brief summary of your cover and is the legal proof needed to tax your car or to present to the police upon request.

There are other types of documentation required to drive a car.

Driving Licence

Upon reaching the age of 16 you can apply for your provisional driving licence. This licence allows you to drive agricultural vehicles and mopeds on the road, but no other vehicle until you reach 17. At 17 you can start learning to drive a car and can drive on the roads if accompanied by an adult aged 21 or over, who has held a full driving licence for three years or more. You must also be included on the vehicle's insurance and display 'L' plates. It is best to seek training from a specialist instructor when learning to drive, as it will improve your chances of passing the driving test, which you can sit at 17.

On passing the driving test you will be issued with a driving licence consisting of two parts – a paper part and a card part. If the police, DVA (Driver and Vehicle Agency) or the courts request your licence you will need to provide both parts. The card is your actual licence and shows your full driving entitlements, including the types of vehicle the licence allows you to drive. The paper part shows other information, such as any endorsements on your licence.

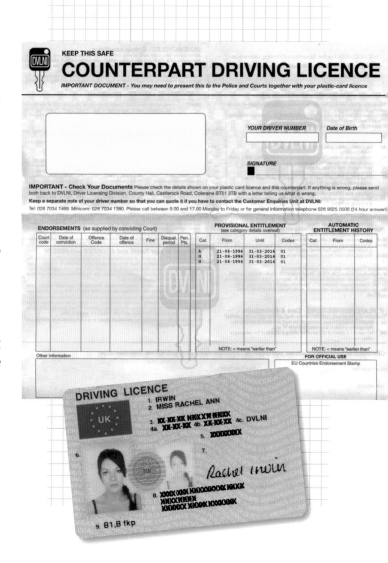

Newly qualified drivers in Northern Ireland must obey the following legal requirements:

1. Display 'R' plates for one year after passing their test.
2. Restrict their speed to 45 mph for one year after passing their test.

The restrictions above do not apply in England. To drive a HGV (heavy goods vehicle), PSV (public service vehicle) or PCV (passenger carrying vehicle), you must be at least 21 years old, hold a full driving licence and sit a specialist driving test.

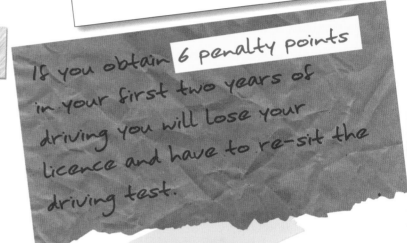

FOR YOUR FOLDER

1. **At what age can you apply for your provisional licence?**
2. **At what age can you drive a moped on the road?**
3. **Name two legal requirements for newly qualified drivers.**
4. **How long does a driver have to display 'R' plates for?**
5. **What happens if a newly qualified driver obtains six penalty points in his or her first two years of driving?**
6. **What do HGV, PSV and PCV stand for?**
7. **What age must you be to drive an HGV vehicle?**

If you obtain 6 penalty points in your first two years of driving you will lose your licence and have to re-sit the driving test.

Road Tax
(vehicle excise licence)

All road vehicles must purchase a vehicle excise licence. A disc should be displayed inside the vehicle windscreen as legal proof of purchase and that the vehicle is allowed to use the roads.

The tax disc displays the following information:
- The expiry date
- The vehicle make and registration
- The price and the tax group

Road tax is obtained by filling in an application form available at your local vehicle licensing office or a post office. You will need to provide your vehicle's insurance certificate, your MOT certificate (if your car is over four years old) and the fee to be paid. You can either tax your vehicle for six months or one year. Prices vary according to each vehicle's age, engine size and exhaust emissions.

Road tax expires on the last day of the month shown on the tax disc. The tax can be renewed up to one month before the expiry date and fourteen days grace will be granted by the DVA after the expiry date. However, the police can impose penalties on vehicles that are not displaying a valid tax disc five days after the actual expiry date. If you do not have a current tax disc, DVA Enforcement Officers have the authority to clamp your car. You will not only have to pay a fee to release your car but you must also pay for the car to be taxed. Some road agencies employed by the DRDNI (Department for Regional Development) and the DOENI (Department for the Environment NI) set up temporary camera stations to read vehicle registrations and check if the vehicle is taxed. The camera's images are proof that vehicles have been driving on the roads without tax.

A **SORN** (statutory off road notification) document can be obtained to declare ownership of a vehicle that is officially 'off the road' and where it will be staying. You will not have to pay road tax for this vehicle as you will not be driving it on the roads.

Source: DVA, www.dvani.gov.uk

FOR YOUR FOLDER

1. What is a vehicle excise licence?
2. Where must a vehicle excise licence be displayed?
3. What information does it display?
4. Where can you obtain a vehicle excise licence from?
5. What is a SORN document?
6. What other documents do you need to produce to obtain a vehicle excise licence?

Tax Book
(vehicle registration document)

The V5 form or tax book lists a vehicle's make, model, colour, date of registration, chassis number, taxation group (class) and its previous owners. These forms and books prove that the vehicle belongs to you and that it has not been stolen or tampered with. The green tax books for Northern Ireland road users started being replaced in 2004 by a V5 registration document. This V5 form is now provided for all vehicle owners in the EU when they register their vehicle for the first time.

MOT

(vehicle test certificate)

All vehicles older than four years old in Northern Ireland must complete an annual MOT test at a government controlled DVA centre. In England all vehicles older than three years old must complete an annual MOT test, which is carried out by designated garages. A vehicle is awarded a MOT certificate as proof that it is in a good condition and safe to drive on the roads. This legal requirement encourages road users to look after their vehicle, ensuring it has regular maintenance and safety checks by a qualified mechanic. The MOT test is only carried out once a year and therefore only tests the vehicle on its condition at this time. However, this comprehensive inspection helps to improve the roadworthiness of older vehicles.

Before taking your vehicle for its MOT test it is wise to have it serviced or checked by a mechanic and to wash it (if underneath your vehicle is too dirty they will not test it). These steps will give your vehicle the best possible chance of passing the test, saving you the cost of a re-test just because your vehicle needed something small fixed. The main checks carried out during the MOT test include the following:

- Seat belts
- Brakes
- Electrics (lights, wipers, horn, indicators)
- Steering and suspension systems
- Tyres
- Exhaust system (including its carbon monoxide and hydrocarbon emissions)

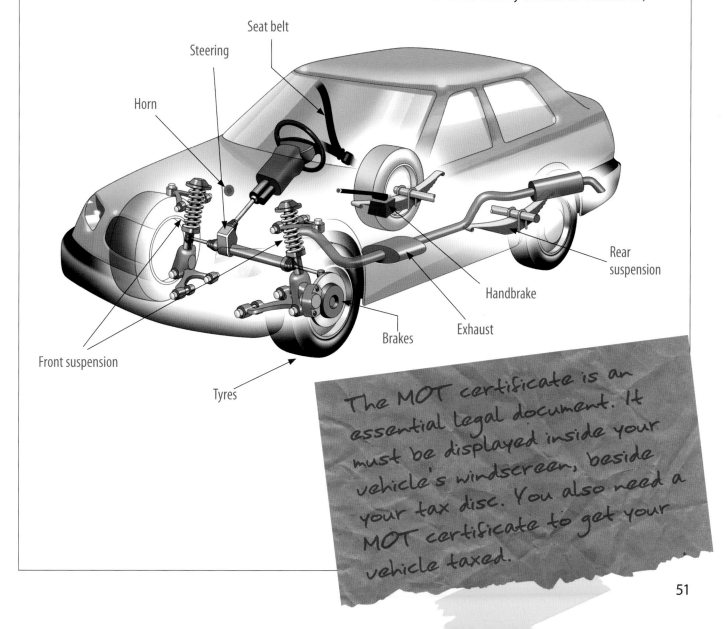

The MOT certificate is an essential legal document. It must be displayed inside your vehicle's windscreen, beside your tax disc. You also need a MOT certificate to get your vehicle taxed.

FOR YOUR FOLDER

1. What is a vehicle registration document and what details does it provide?

2. What two discs must be displayed inside a vehicle windscreen?

3. What are vehicles over four years of age legally required to have and why?

4. What two things could a vehicle owner do to prepare a car for the MOT?

5. Make a list of checks carried out during the MOT.

6. What are the names of the two exhaust gases that are checked?

7. What happens if a vehicle does not pass all the checks?

 THINK

Draw a table similar to the one below. Using the Internet research each of the legal requirements associated with driving. Use this information to fill in the spaces in the table.

Legal requirements	Costs
Road tax/vehicle excise licence	
MOT	
Full driving licence	
Provisional driving licence	
Theory test	
Practical test	
Insurance (average motor insurance for a 17 year old)	+
Total cost of driving	

THE VEHICLE

It is important that all vehicles' operating systems are checked before they are taken onto the road to ensure that they are working correctly. The windscreen wipers must function properly to keep the windscreen clear, assisting visibility. Legal requirements insist that windscreen washers always have fluid in them to clear the windscreen with water or screen wash if it gets dirty. Wipers' blades are made of rubber, and will become worn and need replaced occasionally. It is essential that your vehicle's horn is working in case you need to make people aware of your presence. For example, if a reversing vehicle does not seem to see you, you could sound your horn to warn them that they are too close to your vehicle.

Vehicle lighting improves your vision and allows other road users to see you, especially at night or in poor weather conditions. All lights, both front and rear, including brake lights and indicators, should be checked regularly in case a bulb has blown. Brake lights are essential for letting other motorists know that you are braking. If they are not working properly someone could drive into the back of your vehicle because they do not realise that you are slowing down. Indicators are similarly important because they inform other road users of your intentions.

Efficient brakes allow vehicles to slow down and stop safely. Brake pads cause heat and friction and will eventually wear away because of the constant rubbing against a brake disc or drum. Worn brake pads will make the braking system less efficient, which is dangerous because it will increase stopping distances. Therefore brake pads will need replacing and should be checked at each service by your mechanic. It is also essential that a vehicle's steering is working efficiently to ensure the vehicle travels where you want it to. Tyres that are knocked off line by striking something hard or uneven, such as a pothole or kerb, may cause a vehicle to pull to one side and affect its steering. If you feel the steering pulling to one side you should go to tyre service station to check the balance and alignment of your tyres.

Tyres

Good tyres are essential for the safe motoring of any vehicle and they should be checked regularly to ensure the following:

- There should be no foreign bodies such as nails, stones, thorns or glass stuck in the tyre treads or walls.
- All tyres are the correct tyre pressure. Tyres that are soft (with too little air in them) will make steering more difficult. Tyres that are hard (with too much air in them) can reduce grip with the road surface, making the car bounce. If a hard tyre strikes an object or hump when travelling on an uneven road surface it could puncture or 'blow out'.
- All tyres should be the same pressure to ensure the vehicle is well balanced.
- The tyre treads should be clearly visible. As tyre treads are used to improve grip with the road surface and disperse surface water, it is essential that their depth is sufficient. You can check the tread depth by looking at a depth indicator on the

tyre. If the indicator is still visible the tyre's remaining tread depth is adequate. If it is worn away the tyre needs replaced.

The police sometimes check vehicles' tyre conditions at check points. If any of the tyre's pressure or tread depth is insufficient the vehicle's driver could receive a fine or penalty points.

The legal tread depth for cars, vans and light vehicles is 1.6 mm.

The size of a tyre is sometimes printed on the side wall of a new tyre with information similar to this: 225/40 R18. This means that the tyre has a width of 225 mm, a profile of 40% and fits a rim or alloy with an 18 inch diameter.

Depth Indicator

The legal tread depth for a motorcycle is 1.0 mm.

FOR YOUR FOLDER

1. Name three tyre checks that should be carried out regularly.

2. What effect will driving with soft tyres have on handling a vehicle?

3. What is the purpose of depth indicators on the tyres?

4. What is the legal tyre tread depth for a car?

5. What is the legal tyre tread depth for a motorcycle?

Seat Belts

You **must** always wear a seat belt if one is available, unless you are exempt. You may be exempt if you have a shoulder, chest or arm injury. Your doctor or local hospital can provide a medical exemption certificate, which must be produced by the driver to the police if stopped. If you are stopped by the police and found not to be wearing a seat belt, you or the driver (if not yourself) are likely to receive penalty points or a fine. Adults should be responsible and set a good example to children by always putting on their seat belt. All children should be secured during travel using one of the following child restraints:

- Baby carrier
- Child seat
- Harness or booster seat

You should look at the section on seat belts and child restraints more closely in your Highway Code book.

Summary of the legal requirements

	FRONT SEAT	REAR SEAT	WHO IS RESPONSIBLE?
Driver	Seat belt must be worn		Driver
Child under 3 years of age	Child restraint must be worn	Child restraint must be worn	Driver
Child aged 3–12	Child restraint must be worn	Child restraint must be worn	Driver
Child aged 12–13	Adult seat belt must be worn	Adult seat belt must be worn	Driver
Passenger aged 14 years and over	Seat belt must be worn	Seat belt must be worn	Passenger

FOR YOUR FOLDER

1. State two advantages of wearing seat belts.
2. Who is exempt from wearing seat belts?
3. What are the legal requirements for wearing seat belts in your *Highway Code* book?
4. What are the legal requirements regarding seat belts for children under the age of three?
5. What is considered an appropriate child restraint?

THINK

Using the Internet see if you can find any statistics relating to the regulations about the wearing of seat belts and note them under the following headings:

- Legal requirements
- Accident statistics
- Penalties imposed

TRANSPORT	ADVANTAGES	DISADVANTAGES
TRAIN 	Generally plenty of passenger room; comfortable; can get up and walk about; relaxing; do not have to think about parking; avoid traffic; safer than travelling by car because it travels on its own track and does not come into contact with other vehicles; its larger framework, weight and size, also allow it to withstand greater impacts.	Restricted by train timetable; cost per ride (more than a bus); can be quite full leaving little passenger room; passengers have to get themselves to and from the station; may not be a station near passengers' work/home/destination.

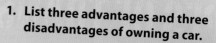

FOR YOUR FOLDER

1. **List three advantages and three disadvantages of owning a car.**

2. **Think of three types of public transport.**

3. **List two advantages and two disadvantages of travelling by bus.**

4. **State one main advantage of a bus lane in towns and cities.**

5. **Why is driving a motorcycle considered to be more dangerous than driving a motor car?**

DEVELOPMENT OF TRANSPORT

Before the introduction of motor vehicles in the nineteenth century people still needed to travel. In the seventeenth and eighteenth centuries stagecoaches pulled by horses were used to carry passengers, and wagons pulled by horses were used to deliver materials and supplies. In the nineteenth century the development of railways saw the first real alternative to horse-drawn vehicles – trains. Trains were popular as they carried larger numbers of passengers, materials and supplies. While the railway network was expanding another mode of power and transport was being developed.

In 1826 the first gas internal combustion road engine was developed. The new road vehicles that used this engine were very popular with the public but not with stagecoach or railway firms, which were losing custom. Local government officials were pressurised to impose higher road tax on steam-powered vehicles and they also introduced the 1865 Highways and Locomotives Act (the Red Flag Act). This act restricted the speed of steam-powered vehicles and a person had to walk in front of each vehicle carrying a red flag so that the vehicle did not break any speed limits. Bicycles were also very popular in the nineteenth century, as they enabled people to travel short distances independently. People travelling long distances to work often used bicycles to get to the nearest railway station.

Development of the motor car

The biggest development in road travel came in 1885 when a German man called Karl Benz produced the first motor car, using an internal combustion engine to run on petrol. With the development of the motor car the law was forced to change and the 1865 Red Flag Act was replaced with The Locomotives on Highways Act 1896. This act set a new speed limit of 14 mph and forced all vehicles to carry a bell or other instrument to warn others of their approach.

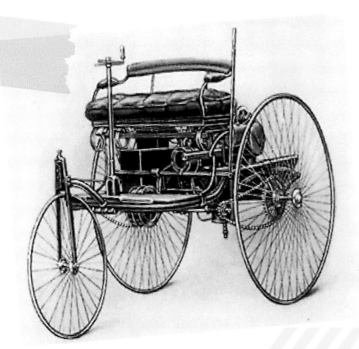

Karl Benz

BENZ PATENT MOTORWAGEN, 1885

Different shapes and makes of motor cars were developed over the years and in 1913 a man called Henry Ford introduced the assembly line. Before, building a single motor car was both expensive and time consuming. The assembly line meant that Ford could mass-produce his motor vehicle, the Ford Model T, as each individual vehicle could be assembled in an hour and a half.

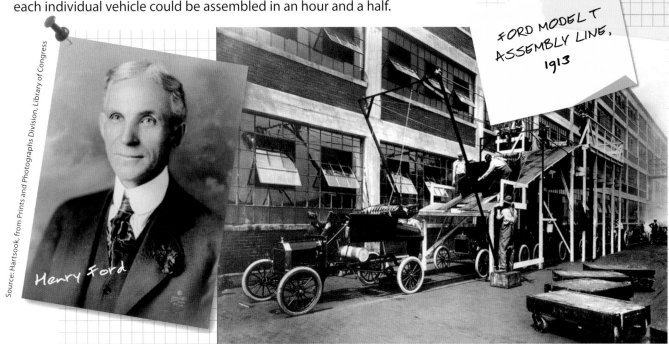

Source: Hartsook, from Prints and Photographs Division, Library of Congress

Henry Ford

FORD MODEL T ASSEMBLY LINE, 1913

Seventeenth century	(1600–1700)	Dust tracks were used by horses and stage coaches.
Eighteenth century	(1700–1800)	New roads were developed with more freedom for horses and stage coaches.
Nineteenth century	(1800–1900)	Railways, steam engines and bicycles were new attractions. The introduction and development of first internal combustion engine. The first motor car was designed by Karl Benz in 1885.
Twentieth century	(1900–2000)	New roads are built to accommodate the development of the motor car. The assembly line and mass production of one vehicle was introduced by Henry Ford. The first motorways were built in the 1950s.
Twenty-first century	(2000–2100)	The development of the modern day motor car with improved technology, comfort and safety features.

Throughout the twentieth century the design and manufacture of motor vehicles gradually improved, with the introduction of hydraulic brakes; safety glass; bumpers; and electric components such as lights, windscreen wipers, speedometers, radios and the horn. Manufacturers today continue to make improvements in the safety, design, technology and comfort of their vehicles to meet the ever increasing demands of the consumer.

The relationship between accident prevention and motor vehicle technology

The vehicle industry is very competitive, with manufacturers mass-producing their products to keep costs as low as possible. Many factors influence the buyer's choice of vehicle including its type, cost, interior design and comfort. However, in all areas of vehicle design and manufacture it is the safety of its occupants and its performance under everyday driving conditions that are given the most attention. The link between accident prevention and motor vehicle technology is a major factor influencing the design of motor vehicles. Car manufacturers are constantly improving and updating their primary and secondary safety features, because safety ratings are high on many consumers' wish lists.

primary safety

Primary safety relates to all the features that help a vehicle perform safely in everyday driving conditions. Some examples are shown below:

- Steering and location of the controls
- Tyres
- Lights and indicators
- Effective wipers

secondary safety

Secondary safety relates to all the features that protect a vehicle's occupants if it is involved in a road traffic collision. Some examples are shown below:

- Air bags
- Seat belts
- Side impact bars (to strengthen the door panels)

These features are described in greater detail in the section entitled 'Methods to reduce accidents' on page 41.

FOR YOUR FOLDER

1. Who designed the first motor car?
2. Draw a block diagram to show how transport has developed over the years.
3. Why do car manufacturers mass-produce their vehicles?
4. What is meant by the term primary safety?
5. List four items of primary safety on a motor vehicle.
6. What is meant by the term secondary safety?
7. List three items of secondary safety on a motor vehicle.

DEVELOPMENT OF THE MODERN ROAD SYSTEM AND TRAFFIC MANAGEMENT

Over 8,000 years ago a typical road was simply a dust or dirt track made by horses and wagons. The introduction of stagecoaches meant that these tracks needed to be widened and flattened to allow the coaches to travel more smoothly. Roads needed constant updating and improving as road traffic increased. It became necessary to build longer lasting roads, with smooth, waterproof surfaces. The introduction of tarmac in 1845 helped to achieve these smooth, waterproof roads. Roads today are built on foundations of concrete and stone, and reinforced with steel mesh to prevent the concrete cracking under the weight of constant traffic. These foundations are coated with tarmac and laid with a slight incline from the centre to the edge of the road, allowing rain water to run into drains situated at the edge. With the ever-increasing population and advancements in technology, the conditions of roads are continually improving. Today there are a number of different types of roads:

- **Motorways** – These are fast moving roads that usually link major cities. They have a number of traffic lanes heading in each direction, with a central barrier or reservation separating the opposing directions. The signs on these roads generally have white lettering on a blue background and the speed limit is usually 70 mph, unless stated differently. The first motorways in the UK were designed and built in the 1950s to help ease traffic flow and to enable motorists to get to their destination quickly and safely. Learner drivers and agricultural vehicles are not allowed to use motorways because of their speed restrictions. Stopping and U-turns are also prohibited, and slip roads are used to enter and exit motorways, allowing traffic to remain travelling at, or to get up to, the required speed.

- **Dual-carriageways** – These are also fast moving roads that link major towns and cities. These roads usually have two traffic lanes heading in each direction, also separated by a central reservation. The right-hand lane is used for fast moving traffic and overtaking. The speed limit is 70 mph unless signs state otherwise.

- **Single-carriageways** – These roads can also be fast moving and are characterised by having no central reservation to separate the lanes of traffic travelling in opposite directions. Speed limits in rural areas are usually 60 mph.

- **Primary routes** – These are used to describe major roads, and can include all types of carriageways. Except for motorways, primary routes have green signs with white letters.

- **Non-primary routes** – These are ordinary town (urban) or country (rural) roads on which we generally drive most frequently. This type of road has signs with black lettering on a white background.

- **Single-track roads** – These are roads with only one traffic lane. If vehicles meet on this type of road one of the vehicles will have to pull into a gap and stop to allow the other to pass. If no gap is available at the meeting place one vehicle will have to reverse back along the road until it reaches a space wide enough to allow the other vehicle to pass.

- **Autostrada** – This is the name given to motorways in Italy. The recommended speed limit on these motorways is 80 mph.

- **Autobahns** – This is the name given to motorways in Germany. The first autobahns were built in the 1930s. The recommended speed limit on these motorways is 130 km/h (80.6 mph) and all signs are blue with white lettering.

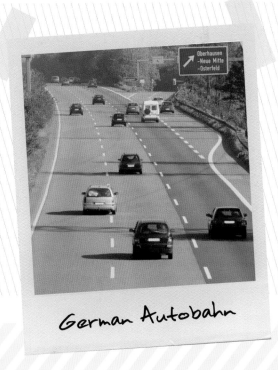

German Autobahn

Unfortunately the upgrading and building of better roads usually encourages more vehicles onto the roads and faster speeds. Traffic congestion is also a common problem in towns, cities and built up areas. A number of important road safety measures have been introduced to ease traffic congestion and keep it flowing. The introduction of parking restrictions and one-way streets in towns and cities have been a welcome addition for many motorists. Pedestrianisation zones are also becoming more common in busy shopping areas to prevent traffic from entering them between the working hours of 8 am and 6 pm. The safety and freedom of all pedestrians is an essential factor in the design of these zones. Usually the only vehicles allowed into these zones are bin lorries and delivery vans, and generally only at designated times, when pedestrian activity is at its lowest. These times are usually before or after the normal working hours of 8 am and 6 pm.

Traffic 'calming measures are an essential environmental factor used to reduce speeding in built-up areas. These are described in greater detail in the section entitled 'Methods to reduce accidents' on page 41 and in your Highway Code book.

speed humps

speed cushions

horizontal deflection

FOR YOUR FOLDER

1. How would you describe a typical road 8,000 years ago?

2. What type of transport used these roads?

3. When were the first motorways built?

4. What colours are the signs and lettering on motorways?

5. What is a central reservation?

6. What does the term 'autostrada' mean?

7. What is meant by the term 'traffic calming'?

8. Name three traffic calming measures?

9. State two advantages of a pedestrianisation zone?

10. At what times are delivery vehicles and bin lorries usually allowed into pedestrianisation zones?

11. What is an autobahn?

SOCIAL AND ENVIRONMENTAL EFFECTS OF POLLUTION

All roads form part of the landscape and the environment, and all of us benefit from them as drivers, passengers, pedestrians or cyclists. The majority of homes have at least one car, if not two. This has an immediate impact on the environment. As the population increases so does the number of vehicles on our roads. Larger volumes of traffic will pollute the air that we breathe and increase noise levels. Increased noise levels can damage people's hearing or disturb people who live close to, or are in hospitals near, busy roads. However, there is a need for good road networks that cater for the large volume of traffic on the roads today.

Unfortunately, the need for new roads can sometimes have unavoidable impacts on the landscape and countryside. Sometimes there is no practical alternative for a proposed road. This can often lead to conflict between land owners, local agencies or businesses who will lose land or business as a result of a new road. A new road may redirect traffic away from certain locations or communities, causing a loss of revenue to filling stations or roadside café's. However, if private lands or grounds are needed for new roads, compensation will be paid to the owners. Many new roads are unfortunately forced to carry traffic through:

- Valued landscapes
- Wildlife habitats and reserves
- Close to historic towns or occasionally sites of scientific and archaeological interest.
- Agricultural land
- Private property – gardens, farm yards, business yards, etc

Before a new road is designed an environmental assessment is carried out to see what effects it could have on people and their environment. The assessment includes:

- The effect of traffic noise
- The effects on agriculture
- The effect on community severance (destruction of services and amenities)
- The effect of air pollution
- The visual impact
- The effect on heritage and conservation areas
- The effect on wildfowl and wildlife
- The effect on pedestrians and cyclists
- The disruption due to construction works
- The views from the road

Environmental experts have developed a number of ways to minimise the destruction of, and disruption to, the environment and the landscape. A few of these are listed below:

- Planting trees and certain seeding flowers that provide both food and cover for birds and small mammals.

- Cutting or lowering roads so that the countryside and visual impact of the landscape is not affected.

The Broadway underpass on the M1 entrance to Belfast in Northern Ireland.

- Constructing or replacing natural features to maintain a pleasing visual picture.

- Building tunnels or underpasses.

- Constructing underground tunnels or underpasses to prevent animals crossing busy roads, and placing nesting boxes under bridges and near road verges.

This wildlife underpass in LA county was constructed to allow animals such as bobcats, coyotes and American badgers to safely cross Harbour Boulevard. Harbour Boulevard is a four lane road cutting through land managed by Puente Hills Landfill Native Habitat Preservation Authority.

FOR YOUR FOLDER

1. List three environmental factors that influence the design of a new road.

2. List three ways in which environmental experts can minimise the destruction to the environment.

3. How can animals be stopped from crossing the road?

4. List one example of how a new road has changed the environment in some way near your home.

5. How can the building of new roads affect air pollution?

6. Why is it important to plant new trees and replace as many natural features as possible when building new roads?

Effects of pollution

Large volumes of traffic in our society today have played a major part in the increased levels of pollution. Exposure to air pollution can cause premature death and illnesses. There are a number of different types of exhaust pollutants:

- **Carbon monoxide** is a type of gas in the atmosphere that, when inhaled, restricts the flow of oxygen around the body. This affects the central nervous system, impairing physical co-ordination, vision and judgement.

- **Nitrogen oxides** are formed during the burning of petrol in the engine. These gases can cause breathing problems such as bad coughs, runny noses and sore throats.

- **Carbon dioxide** is a major greenhouse gas that seriously effects climate change.

- **Hydrocarbons** are emitted from vehicle exhausts as unburned fuel. These gases can cause coughing, sneezing, lung and eye irritation.

- **Sulphur dioxide** is a gas emitted from a vehicle's exhaust after diesel fuel has been burned. The build up of this gas in the atmosphere causes acid rain. The air after a shower of rain still contains particles of sulphur, which can affect breathing and cause lung problems.

- **Lead** is a dangerous exhaust pollutant that can cause serious damage to the kidneys, liver and reproductive organs. It has been shown to contribute to behavioural problems and impair people's concentration.

Efforts to reduce pollution

In an attempt to reduce exhaust gases, the majority of car manufacturers have incorporated catalytic converters into their exhaust systems. These converters are used to remove carbon monoxide, hydrocarbons and nitrogen oxides from exhaust gases. Government officials across the world advised all vehicle manufacturers to insert catalytic converters into all vehicles to improve air quality and reduce the amount of harmful gases released into the atmosphere. These gases affect the environment; wildlife; cause climate change; and have lead to an increase in the number of human health problems, such as respiratory breathing problems that affect the lungs and increase the risk of asthma.

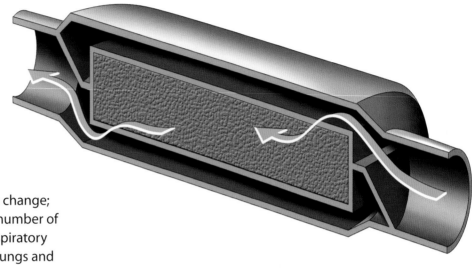

Certain measures have been taken by the UK Government to try and minimise the effects of pollution. Legislation was introduced in 2001 to try and discourage motorists from driving vehicles with high exhaust emissions and to encourage the purchase of less polluting models. Every vehicle was given its own specific road tax grouping, ranging from A–G (A the least expensive and G the most expensive) and costing from £0 to £400, depending on the amount of exhaust emissions. In April 2009 these tax groupings increased from A–M, increasing taxation on high polluting vehicles. The higher the exhaust emissions, the more expensive the road tax. Sports cars, 4x4s, vehicles with bigger engines or twin exhausts will all have high tax groupings because of the large amounts of exhaust emissions that they emit. This legislation persuades motorists to think twice about the type of vehicle they drive, reducing unnecessary exhaust emissions and therefore damage to the environment. For example, generally a couple with one child will not need a large,

4x4 jeep to leave the child to school and to do the shopping. A smaller vehicle would emit less exhaust gases into the atmosphere, would use less fuel and have a lower road tax, therefore making it more economical to run.

The introduction of lead-free petrol has helped to reduce exhaust emissions. Engines need to run at their highest level and require good performance fuel to do so. Four-star petrol used to be a slightly better quality fuel than unleaded and therefore motorists were more likely to purchase it. The introduction of a new super unleaded fuel, LRP (Lead Replacement Fuel), has made replacing the more damaging, lead carrying, four-star fuel more practical. Filling stations no longer sell four-star petrol.

Exhaust gases are not the only forms of pollution. Some motorists throw litter out of their vehicles while driving, which can injure wildlife and spoil the countryside.

As already discussed on page 65, noise pollution is a common problem, especially in towns and cities. Busy roads, railways and airports close to residential areas can annoy inhabitants. The occupants of these houses sometimes have to spend more money on sound insulation to drown out external noise.

FOR YOUR FOLDER

1. Why is air pollution from exhaust gases a very serious problem?
2. List some exhaust gases.
3. What effect does carbon monoxide have on the body?
4. What exhaust gas is a major contributor to climate change?
5. How would you describe hydrocarbons and what do they do to the body?
6. How do vehicle manufacturers help to reduce exhaust emissions?

FOR YOUR FOLDER

7. What exhaust gases do catalytic converters remove?
8. What measures have been taken to remove lead as a major pollutant?
9. What do the letters LRP stand for?
10. Apart from exhaust gases, name two other types of pollution that motorists and their vehicles can cause.

MOTORING LAWS

All pupils should be able to give a brief explanation to demonstrate their knowledge of the following motoring laws.

The Highways and Locomotives Act (The Red Flag Act) 1865

- this act required three persons to drive or conduct every locomotive propelled by steam or any other power (except animal power).
- at least one of these persons should walk at least 60 yards in front and carry a red flag to warn riders and drivers of horses.

- this act set the speed limit at 4 mph and at 2 mph through a city, town or village.

The Locomotives on Highways Act 1896

Following the development of the motor car:

- this act exempted light locomotives (vehicles under three tons unladen weight, propelled by mechanical power, including petroleum) from the 1865 restrictions.
- such vehicles had to carry a bell or other instrument to warn of their approach.
- the speed limit for these vehicles was set at 14 mph.

The Motor Car Act 1903

This act:

- adopted the term 'motor car'
- introduced the requirement to register a motor car with a county or borough council.
- introduced registration (number) plates.
- introduced licensing of drivers by county or borough councils.
- set the licence fee.
- set the qualifying age for a motor car licence at 17 and the age for a motorcycle licence at 14.
- introduced suspension, disqualification and endorsement of licences.

The Road Traffic Act 1930

This act introduced, among other things:

- provisional licences and driving tests.
- speed limits.
- compulsory third party insurance.
- driving offences (dangerous, reckless and careless driving, and driving under the influence of drink or drugs).
- provisions relating to the issue of the *Highway Code*.

The Road Traffic Act (Northern Ireland) 1955

This act brought legislation in Northern Ireland into line with that in Great Britain and introduced:

- provisional licences, driving tests and regulations regarding physical fitness and age qualification (17 for car drivers and 16 for motorcyclists).
- driving offences (dangerous and careless driving, driving under the influence of drink or drugs and driving while uninsured).
- disqualification from driving.
- offences by pedestrians, cyclists and motorcyclists.
- the issue of the *Highway Code*.

The Road Traffic (Seat Belts) (NI) Order 1981

- this order empowered the Department of Education to make regulations requiring adults to wear seat belts in the front and rear seats, and children to wear seat belts in the front seats.
- regulations relating to the front seats were introduced on 31 January 1983.
- regulations relating to adults in the rear were introduced on 1 July 1991.

The Motor Vehicles (Wearing of Rear Seat Belts by Children) (NI) Order 1989

- this order required children to wear seat belts in the rear and that the regulations became operative on 1 September 1989.

The Road Traffic (Amendment) (NI) Order 1991

- this order made fresh provision in respect of offences arising out of driving or being in charge of a motor vehicle while under the influence of drink or drugs.
- including an obligatory minimum disqualification period of 12 months and the requirement to resit the driving test, if convicted.

The Road Traffic Offenders (NI) Order 1996

This order introduced a system of penalty points, as follows:

- road traffic offences are separated into those which involve obligatory

MOTORING LAWS...

endorsement and those which are not endorsable.

- endorsable offences carry a number or range of penalty points which are endorsed on the counterpart of the licence in all situations where a court, convicting a person of an offence involving obligatory endorsement, does not order disqualification.

- where a driver accumulates 12 or more points within a three year period, he or she is subject to a period of disqualification.

- this is for a period of six months, but this can be increased to one or two years depending on the number of previous disqualifications in the preceding three years.

The Road Traffic (NI) Order 2007

This order introduced a range of measures, as follows:

- penalty points for non-wearing of seat belts and for using a hand-held mobile phone while driving.

- power to courts to make use of retraining courses for drink/drive offences.

- an on-the-spot fixed penalty deposit scheme and powers to issue fixed penalties to drivers without a UK licence (to prevent foreign drivers escaping penalties by leaving the country).

- police powers to seize and dispose of vehicles if driven without insurance.

- a new system of endorsement which will allow EU drivers to avail of the fixed penalty system rather than having to appear in court.

- the vehicle test (MOT) disc to be displayed on the windscreen.

- an approved test assistant to help an applicant during the driving test if the applicant has hearing difficulties or difficulties understanding or responding to instructions, for example language translators.

Source: Appendix A, CCEA Motor Vehicle and Road User Studies Specification (2001)

Chapter Four

MOTORING MATHEMATICS

BUYING A VEHICLE

Most teenagers passing their driving test at 17 years old would like to own their own car so that they can have complete freedom and independence. Cars seem more expensive to buy whenever you are young. You may still be in full time education, with only a part-time job, or you may be an apprentice, having only started out in your chosen career. Its takes a few years to gather up enough money to buy a vehicle. Some people are fortunate enough that their parents include them on their insurance for a couple of years. Others might even have a car bought for them but the majority of teenagers will have to save to buy their own. There are many factors influencing the overall cost of owing a vehicle and there are many opportunities for borrowing money. However, you need to be careful that you can comfortably pay back any money you borrow and not get yourself into any difficulty with debt. The cost of borrowing needs to be carefully considered by looking at the positives and negatives of each method.

The term 'straight sale' simply means buying a vehicle without trading in another against it. The buying of brand new vehicles are normally straight sales. New vehicles are usually bought with warranties, which cover them for a set period of time, usually years, against mechanical faults. If your vehicle is deemed to have a serious mechanical fault while under warranty most manufacturers will replace it if the fault cannot be sorted out by the specialist manufacturer. Unfortunately, with buying a second-hand vehicle, especially if it is older than two or three, they will not usually be covered by warranty and you can never be sure how long they will last.

When purchasing a vehicle you should always ask to see the tax book or V5 form to see how many previous owners the vehicle has had. A vehicle with numerous owners may be an indicator of a troublesome vehicle. You should also ask if the vehicle has a valid MOT certificate, as this document indicates roadworthiness. Some vehicle owners will trade their old vehicle in against a new one to help reduce costs. Other people

MOTORING COSTS

would rather buy privately than go to a car dealer. Dealers are always looking to get their percentage profit out of the vehicle; therefore it can be cheaper to buy privately. A dealer's reputation is in the back of most people's minds when looking for a second-hand vehicle, as information such as mileage can be misleading if tampered with. It is very important that you give a second-hand vehicle a thorough examination before purchasing it. It is also always wise to seek a second opinion, even from your mechanic, before committing yourself to buy.

If you can afford a brand new vehicle this has a few advantages. The vehicle should be in perfect, roadworthy condition when purchased and therefore will not legally require an MOT test for its first four years. If driven and maintained with care it should not need very many repairs in that time and should have fewer running costs than an older car. The main disadvantage of buying a new car is simply the cost, which will be much more than that of a second-hand purchase. However, banks and credit companies will often allow monthly repayments to make purchasing a new vehicle more manageable.

There are four main costs associated with owning a vehicle:

1. **Purchasing costs** – how much and what method is used to pay for the vehicle.

2. **Standing costs** – what legal documents are required before a driver or vehicle can use the roads.

3. **Running costs** – how much does it cost to keep a vehicle on the road.

4. **Additional costs** – these are hidden costs that many motorists forget about.

Purchasing costs

When buying a vehicle you can pay for it using ready cash that you have saved up over a period of time. This is the cheapest option for buying a vehicle but it does take time to save the money. Not everyone is in a position to pay cash for a vehicle and may therefore need to borrow money.

There are many different banks, credit facilities and finance companies all willing to lend money but at a cost. This cost will depend on the monthly rate or on the interest being charged on the amount borrowed. If you borrow money for buying a vehicle you will have to pay interest back on the loan, which will increase the overall cost. This interest is usually known as 'APR' (Annual Percentage Rate). The APR will tell you how expensive the loan will be and how much interest will be charged each year. These repayments will be made monthly. Loans taken out on 'HP' (Hire Purchase) from HP companies often have a higher APR than loans from banks. It is

FOR YOUR FOLDER

1. What is meant by the term 'straight sale'?

2. What is meant by the term 'vehicle under warranty'?

3. What two documents should you ask to see when purchasing a second-hand vehicle?

4. Why would some vehicle owners trade in their old vehicle against a newer model?

5. Why are some people cautious of buying an older, second-hand vehicle from a car dealer?

Standing costs

These costs are legal requirements, in the form of documentation, to prove that a vehicle is legally entitled to use the roads.

- Insurance is usually the most expensive of these costs and is renewed each year. A certificate of insurance is the legal proof needed.

- Any vehicle driver using the roads must pass the official driving test. A driving licence is the official documentation that proves that a driver has passed this test. The cost to sit the theory test in Northern Ireland, in 2009, was £28.50 and the practical driving test was around £55. Both parts must be passed to obtain a driver's licence. The cost of driving lessons (in 2009) was approximately £23–£25.

- Road tax is another legal cost that has to be renewed every year. A tax disc is produced and must be displayed on the inside windscreen of the vehicle.

therefore important that you shop around for the best loan deal, as APR rates will vary. Bank loans are usually the cheapest form of borrowing because interest rates vary and are only charged on the opening balance of the loan. Loans borrowed from finance companies will require you to pay a percentage cost for a vehicle up front and the interest will then be charged on the remaining amount. For example, if you had to pay 20% of a vehicle costing £10000, you would have to pay £2000 up front and then pay a monthly interest rate on the remaining £8000. Using credit facilities enables you to pay for your vehicle monthly over a period of years. This may take the financial pressure of you at the time of buying the vehicle but in the long-term the overall cost of the vehicle will work out more than the original price. Some cars dealers will offer deals to newly qualified drivers, such as free insurance for a set period of years, to encourage them to buy a brand new vehicle.

Some people may wish to lease a vehicle, which means that they are renting a vehicle for a number of years. What they are really paying for is the amount that the vehicle de-values during each year of the lease. Some people may make a down payment at the start of a lease to reduce the size of their monthly payments. The two main advantages of leasing are the lower monthly payments and the opportunity to have a new vehicle every few years.

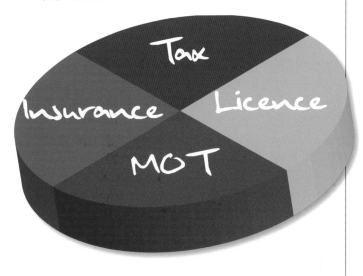

- Vehicles over four years of age must pass an annual MOT inspection. A MOT disc is produced and must also be displayed on the inside windscreen of the vehicle. The cost to MOT a vehicle in 2009 was £30.50 but this does not include the cost of preparing the vehicle. It is wise to have a mechanic to service or check over your vehicle and carry out the necessary repairs to ensure the vehicle has the best possible chance of passing the test. Depending on how well the vehicle is looked after these mechanical costs vary, but they can be quite expensive.

- Motorists also forget about the hidden cost of depreciation. This is the amount that your vehicle decreases each year that you own it.

Running costs

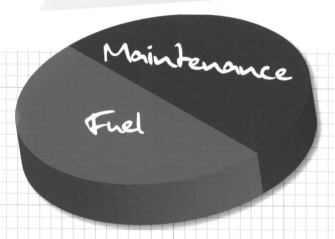

These are the everyday costs that are needed to run a vehicle. The most expensive of these costs is purchasing fuel. Some vehicles are more economical with fuel than others. Factors that can influence fuel usage are the size of the engine, acceleration, speed, and distance of journey. Another running cost is the cost of getting your car serviced and this is advised every 10,000 miles to ensure the best performance from your vehicle. Vehicles regularly need servicing to ensure the full safety of its occupants. Such repairs or replacements might include oil, air or fuel filters; tyres; lights; brake pads; clutch cables; and exhausts. Tyres and replacement bulbs are some of the more regular replacements needed. Owning a troublesome vehicle can be very costly, so it is very important to look after your vehicle to ensure that it runs as

smoothly as possible. Servicing in a garage can be quite expensive. Not only do the parts have to be paid for but the mechanic's time or his labour must be paid for also. For this reason many people, with sufficient knowledge and ability, carry out what DIY repairs they can do themselves to try and reduce the overall cost of servicing.

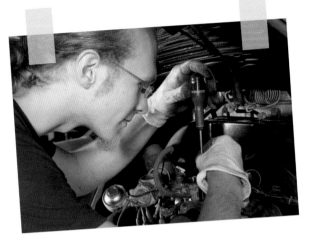

To make running cost payments more manageable some people will set up monthly accounts, for example with fuel companies, so that they can fill their vehicle when needed without having to pay immediately. A monthly statement would then be sent out requesting payment and showing the number of litres purchased. Alternatively, direct debits can also be set up. This allows payments to be taken out of an account on an agreed date each month. Credit cards can also be used to make payments but these generally accrue a lot of interest if the balance is not paid off every month. Some businesses may offer inducements on fuel or parts. Inducements are incentives, usually a reduced price, used to encourage customers to purchase another product or service from the same company.

Additional costs

There are a few other costs that may add to the expense of owning a vehicle, such as parking fees and garaging. Unfortunately some motorists may even pick up fines for parking and speeding, which can add to the cost of motoring. If you decide to take money from an investment (savings) to buy your car, you will lose the interest you would have earned on that investment, as well as the depreciation in the value of the car. This is known as interest on capital investment.

The cost of clothing and footwear, especially for cyclists and motorcyclists, can be quite expensive. Leather and padded clothes to protect the rider can be pricey, as can the essential safety items, such as helmets and reflective gear. The cost of cleaning and lubricating materials and liquids also needs budgeted for. Similarly, if you plan to add a lot of extras to your car, remember CD players, alloy wheels, spoilers, exhausts will all add up!

How to buy a vehicle

1. Never rush into a purchase. Always check local papers, Internet websites and car dealers to see if a vehicle is similarly and reasonably priced elsewhere.

2. Try to take someone experienced with you. A second opinion is priceless.

3. Always view a vehicle in daylight.

4. Check the tax book or V5 form for the number of previous owners and check if the vehicle has an MOT certificate.

5. Check the mileage. The service book should show the mileage at the last service and the MOT certificate should also show this. Check the tyres.

6. Carry out a thorough inspection of the bodywork for rust and dints.

7. Start the vehicle, take it for a test drive, and try all the gears and electrics.

8. Check under the bonnet for a clean engine, clear of oil and leaks. Also check under the vehicle for signs of rust, wear and tear, and leaks.

9. Check that all seat belts fasten and that the inside of the vehicle is in a clean and healthy condition.

10. Ask plenty of questions about the vehicle and always try to negotiate a cheaper price.

FOR YOUR FOLDER

1. What are the two most common methods of purchasing a vehicle?

2. What does HP stand for?

3. Briefly explain how buying a vehicle through a finance company works.

4. Name four standing costs that must be covered by a vehicle owner.

5. What is meant by the term depreciation?

FOR YOUR FOLDER

6. What are running costs?

7. Make a list of the typical running costs of a vehicle.

8. How often is it recommended that you get your vehicle serviced?

9. List four additional costs that can add to the expense of owning a vehicle.

10. List four main points to remember when buying a second-hand vehicle.

CALCULATING COSTS

In order to keep your motoring costs as low as possible there are a number of ways that you can adapt your driving to save fuel. Fuel consumption is the most expensive running cost and a number of situations can be avoided to reduce it. You should:

- avoid unnecessary and short trips in your vehicle.

- drive with care, avoid sudden acceleration and sharp braking. Sharp braking will increase tyre wear, reducing grip and increasing braking distances.

- use air conditioning only when it is absolutely necessary as it increases fuel consumption by about 10%.

- ensure your tyres are at the correct pressure so that your vehicle is easy to steer and handle. Good tyres improve a vehicle's performance and help reduce fuel consumption.

- use higher gears and keep to speed limits to save fuel.

These tips will also help a vehicle to perform better on the roads, save fuel through careful driving and increase the MPG (miles per gallon). MPG is a method used to measure how many miles a vehicle can travel on one gallon of fuel. To calculate average speeds for a journey the total distance is divided by the total time. Keeping at an average speed over an entire journey saves fuel and therefore helps to reduce running costs. Some vehicles perform better than others and will therefore travel a greater distance than others on one gallon of fuel. It is a good idea to ask about the fuel consumption of a vehicle before purchasing it, as you may be considering buying a vehicle that uses a lot of fuel. Statistics have shown that if all vehicles were driven at half the average speed we would save 75% on fuel consumption. Therefore if we drive our vehicles carefully and at the correct speed limits, we could reduce the fuel consumption.

Careful drivers will ultimately reduce maintenance costs by avoiding harsh braking and steering. Speeding drivers will use more fuel and increase braking and stopping distances. These increases will accelerate tyre wear and reduce the effectiveness of the brake pads, parts of the steering and the suspension system. More regular garage visits and maintenance repairs will probably be needed as a result, increasing their vehicles' running costs.

Travel graphs are used to calculate time, distance, speed and to illustrate a road user's journey. They can also be used to calculate average speeds for different sections of a route and to illustrate more than one journey on each graph. The graph opposite gives information on the distance of a cyclist from his home and the type of questions that can be asked on a GCSE paper.

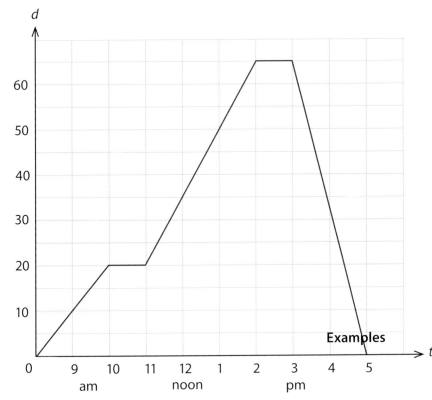

a) When did the cyclist leave home?

b) When did the cyclist return home?

c) How far from home was he at 11 am?

d) How far from home was he at 2 pm?

e) How far from home was he at 3 pm?

f) How far from home was he at 5 pm?

g) At what times did he stop for a rest?

h) Work out his speed from:

   (i)   8 am to 9 pm

   (ii) 12 pm to 2 pm

   (iii) 3 pm to 5 pm

i) Between what times was the cyclist travelling most quickly?

Distance (km) (y-axis)

Time of the day (x-axis)

Examples

Examples 1

A Peugeot 107 is priced in the auto trader magazine at £5799. Purchasers must also pay an indemnity fee of £51, a number plate surcharge of £40 and twelve months' road tax of £110.

a) *What is the total cost of the vehicle?*

b) *Calculate the cost per month over 36 months, if there is a 20% deposit and interest is charged at 15% per annum (assume that all interest is calculated at the start).*

a

Cost of vehicle = **£5799 + £51 + £40 + £110 = £6000**

b

Deposit = 20% of cost of vehicle = $\dfrac{6000 \times 20}{100}$ = **£1200**

Cost interest will be charged on = cost of vehicle - deposit = **£6000 – £1200 = £4800**

Interest per annum (year) = 15% of cost interest will be charged on = $\dfrac{4800 \times 15}{100}$ = **£720**

• • •

1...

Total interest charged over 36 months
= interest per annum × 3 years = **£720 × 3 = £2160**

Total cost of vehicle (including interest) **= £4800 + £2160 = £6960**

The cost per month =
total cost of vehicle (including interest) ÷ 36 months =
£6960 ÷ 36 = £193.33

2

A car costs £15500. If I pay cash I will receive a discount of 10% plus cash back of £1000.

How much extra will I pay if I use vehicle finance, on the full purchase price, with a 20% deposit and 36 monthly payments of £395 per month?

Discount = 10% of £15500 = $\dfrac{£15500 \times 10}{100} = £1550$

Cash cost = car cost − discount − cash back =
£15500 − £1550 − £1000 = £12950

Deposit = 20% of car cost = $\dfrac{£15500 \times 20}{100} = £3100$

Total cost of monthly repayments = 36 monthly payments at £395 =
36 × £395 = £14220

Finance cost = deposit + 36 monthly payments =
£3100 + £14220 = £17320

Extra paid with vehicle finance = finance cost − cash cost =
£17320 − £12950 = £4370

3

A new Vauxhall Vectra 1.7 TDI costs £22145

a) *Calculate its value after one year if it loses 20% in the first 12 months.*

b) *Calculate the % depreciation over 3 years, if its value drops to £13287 over that period.*

a

Loss in first 12 months = 20% of cost = $\dfrac{£22145 \times 20}{100}$ = £4429

Value after one year
= cost – loss in first year = **£22145 – £4429 = £17716**

b

Dropped value = $\dfrac{\text{value after 3 years}}{\text{original price}} \times 100$

$= \dfrac{13287}{22145} \times 100 = 60\%$

If the original price = 100%
Then the dropped price = 60%

Percentage depreciation = **100% – 60% = 40%**

FOR YOUR FOLDER

1. A new Audi TT costs £27000. You have asked for a personalised number plate costing £75 and a set of Audi alloy wheels costing £450 to be fitted. You will leave a deposit of £5000 and use vehicle finance to pay the remaining sum over 5 years.

   a) Calculate the total cost of the vehicle.

   b) Calculate the cost of the monthly payments over 5 years.

2. A Renault Megane is priced in the auto trader magazine at £7000. Purchasers must also pay an indemnity fee of £67.00 and twelve months road tax of £185.00

   a) What is the total cost of the vehicle?

   b) Calculate the cost per month, over 60 months, if there is a 30% deposit and interest is charged at 17.5%.

FOR YOUR FOLDER

3. A driver travels at an average speed of 56 mph for 3 hours.

   a) How far has the vehicle travelled?

   b) A motorist travels at an average speed of 50 mph for 2 hours and spends 3 hours travelling the remaining 60 miles.

   (i) What is the total distance travelled?

   (ii) What is the average speed for the whole journey?

4. In the cooling system of a car engine anti-freeze and water have to be mixed at a ratio of 1:4. If 0.5 litres of anti-freeze is to be used, how much water must be added?

Chapter Five

ACCIDENT PROCEDURES

INVOLVEMENT IN AN ACCIDENT

Road accidents can take many shapes and forms. In all cases the driver must stop at the scene to report the accident. They may involve:

- **Vehicles**
- **Pedestrians**
- **Cyclists**
- **Animals**
- **Property, signs or trees**

If involved in a serious accident all personnel involved must remain at the scene and the police should be contacted. On the police's arrival all occupants have a legal obligation to give their personal details. In some instances motorists may not send for the police and may sort damages out between themselves. This will happen only if the party at fault accepts responsibility, no occupants are injured, all parties are agreed and the cost to repair damages is deemed to be affordable. Motorists may wish to do this to avoid involving their insurance companies, which could result in a higher insurance premium the next year and a loss of their no claims bonus. However, the accident must still be reported to the police within twenty-four hours. The information that needs to be shared and exchanged at the scene of an accident is as follows:

- The name and addresses of all parties involved.
- The personal details of the vehicle owner.
- The vehicle registration number.

This information should be given at the accident scene and if not exchanged then it must be reported to the police within twenty-four hours. Motorists will also be asked to produce their insurance documentation and the driver could be charged with 'Hit and Run' if they delay notifying the police unnecessarily.

Insurance companies will advise you never to accept responsibility for an accident. If you do not admit that the accident was your fault they may be able to legally defend your driving. If they successfully prove that the accident was not your fault they will not have to pay for the damages caused to the other parties involved. Insurance companies cannot proceed with a claim if the accident has not been reported to the police. In some instances the police may not come out to the scene. However, they will always visit the scene if someone has been injured or if the vehicles are badly damaged, cannot be moved and are causing a road obstruction. If the police do not come out and you think that insurance companies may have to be involved, it is wise to take a photograph of the scene, especially if you are not at fault.

POST-ACCIDENT PROCEDURE

Most people do not know what to do upon witnessing an accident, merely looking on horrified and shocked. However, the minutes following an accident are often critical as an injured person's chances of survival may be at risk. A person who knows exactly what to do may save a life and possibly give first aid treatment. This person should be able to organise the following procedures in a calm and constructive manner. There are five main priorities:

Secure the accident scene

This involves **warning other road users** that an accident has happened. Use your hazard warning lights and if possible place a warning triangle at least 45 metres in front of the scene. You should also remember to **protect yourself**, ensuring you are easy to see. This can be achieved by wearing fluorescent or bright materials and by carrying a torch to wave down oncoming traffic.

Summon help from the emergency services - dial 999

Emergency services:

- Police
- Ambulance
- Fire Brigade

Tell them:

- The location of the accident.
- The number of injured victims.
- If there is anyone trapped.
- Whether there is any risk of fire.
- How many vehicles are involved (if any).

On motorways emergency phones can be found by following arrows marked alongside the carriageway. They will put you directly through to the police.

Check that vehicles are safe to approach

Be aware of fuel leaks as any spark could cause an explosion.

Check that vehicles are safe

There are two main tasks that should be carried out:

- **Switch off the ignition.**
- **Put the handbrake on.**

If it is not possible to put the handbrake on, the wheels should be choked with stones or wood to prevent the vehicle from moving, especially on a hill. You should also insist that nobody smokes. If a fire breaks out, try to tackle it with a fire extinguisher or smother it with a blanket. If it gets out of hand, only then should you try to remove the personnel.

Investigate casualties

Always check individuals in a vehicle who are quiet to begin with. The first aid priorities are:

Make sure the person is conscious – A person may be unconscious if unresponsive to your voice or gentle shaking. However, do not shake a casualty that may have a neck or back injury.

Make sure the person is breathing properly – Check the casualty's breathing and ensure that blood, vomit or the tongue are not blocking the air passage. If the casualty is not breathing commence emergency resuscitation to keep the heart pumping blood around the body, especially to the brain. If the brain is deprived of oxygen for more than four minutes permanent damage could occur. The most effective method of resuscitation is mouth-to-mouth, which is performed by completing the following steps:

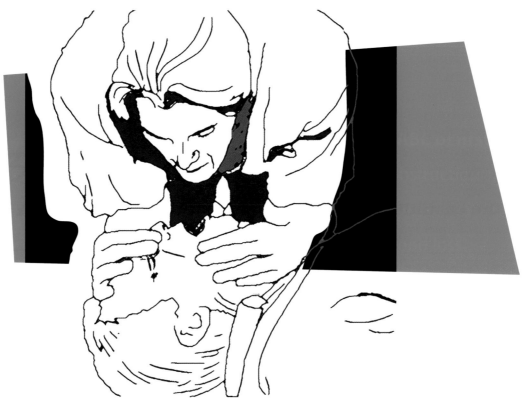

1. Take a deep breath, pulling air back into your lungs.
2. Pinch the casualty's nostrils with your fingers.
3. Seal your lips around the casualty's mouth.
4. Blow into the casualty's lungs until the chest rises.
5. Remove your mouth and watch for the chest falling.
6. Repeat this process until the casualty begins to breath again unassisted or the emergency services arrive.

PRECAUTIONS

Realistic road users will always be prepared for the unexpected, as their vehicle may break down or be involved in an accident at some time during their driving lifetime. This could happen at any time so it is important to be prepared and carry the following items:

- A complete set of replacement bulbs
- A notebook and pen
- A torch
- A fire extinguisher
- A warning triangle
- Reflective/fluorescent bands or jacket
- A first aid kit containing bandages
- A mobile phone

FOR YOUR FOLDER

1. What is the first thing a passer-by should do at the scene of an accident?

2. List in order the five main steps that should be followed at the scene of an accident.

3. What information should be given to the emergency services?

4. How would you contact the emergency services?

5. Make a list of items that would be useful at the scene of an accident.

6. What is a contused wound?

7. What is a lacerated wound?

8. What is the ABC of first aid?

9. What is the BBC of first aid?

Chapter Six

MOTOR VEHICLE TECHNOLOGY

When designing and manufacturing vehicles different manufacturing companies will have their own unique shapes and designs. However, they all must make sure that their vehicles keep the occupants safe, comfortable and perform safely on the roads. The frame or design of a vehicle consists of two main parts, within which a number of systems are built or connected: **the vehicle body** and **the vehicle chassis.**

The body can be defined as the skeleton or shell that holds all the vehicle systems together. It must be built to withstand natural elements, such as adverse weather conditions, and also to protect its occupants in the event of an accident. For example, vehicle doors have side impact bars built into them so that they will not buckle if hit with considerable force. The chassis is simply a strong steel frame underneath the floor of a vehicle. Its function is to support the vehicle's bodywork and engine.

UNDERSTANDING THE CAR

The car is split up into a number of different parts or systems. This diagram shows the main parts:

- **Engine**
- **Cooling system**
- **Exhaust system**

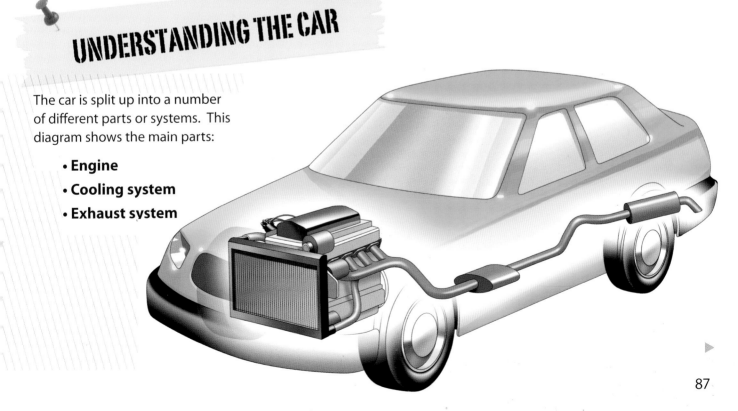

The transmission system

- **Engine**
- **Clutch**
- **Gearbox**
- **Final drive**

Steering

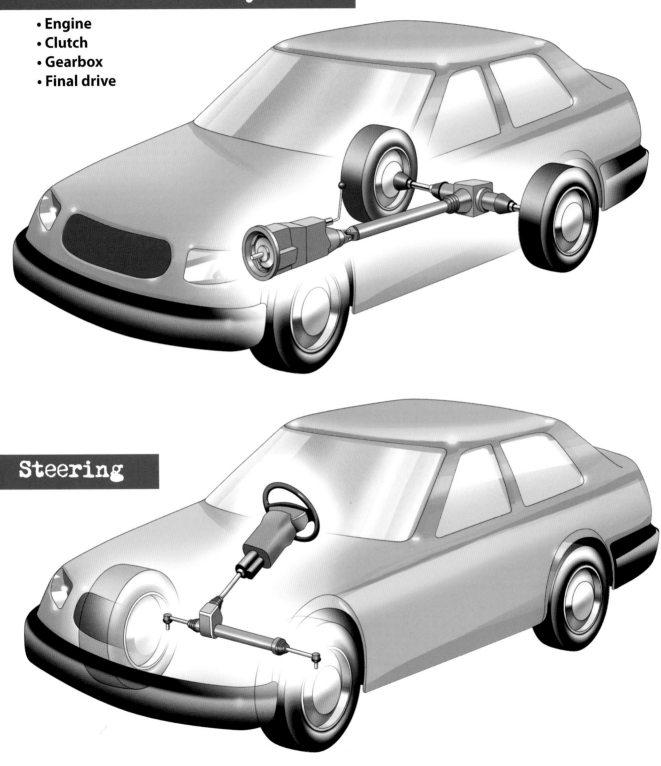

Suspension system

– absorbs shocks, bumps and
jolts caused by the road surface.

Electrical system

- **Charging system**
- **Ignition system**
- **Starting system**

– lights, heater, windscreen wipers, radio, etc

FOR YOUR FOLDER

1. How is the piston connected to the crankshaft?

2. What component does the piston move up and down inside?

3. What two components are attached to the connecting rod?

4. What is the function of the gudgeon pin?

5. What is the function of the two top piston rings?

6. What is the function of the bottom piston ring?

FOR YOUR FOLDER

7. Why does the side of the cylinder need to be lubricated with oil?

8. Where is the cylinder head found?

9. What are the cylinders?

10. What is the function of the timing chain?

11. What two components form the largest part of the engine?

12. What two components is the timing chain connected to?

INTERNAL COMBUSTION ENGINES

There are three types of reciprocating internal combustion engines:

- *The spark ignition four-stroke combustion cycle*
- *The spark ignition two-stroke combustion cycle*
- *The compression ignition four-stroke cycle (diesel engine)*

These three engines all have one thing in common. They all convert reciprocating motion to rotary motion because in each cylinder the piston moves up and down in linear motion, causing the crankshaft, to which the pistons are connected, to turn in rotary motion. This turning motion is then transferred to the gearbox.

THE FOUR-STROKE CYCLE
(The spark-ignition four-stroke cycle)

Induction

The piston moves down in the cylinder. Springs attached to the camshaft open the inlet valve to allow the fuel into the cylinder.

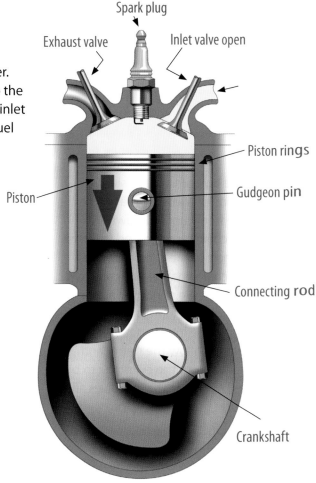

Spark plug

Exhaust valve

Inlet valve open

Piston rings

Piston

Gudgeon pin

Connecting rod

Crankshaft

98

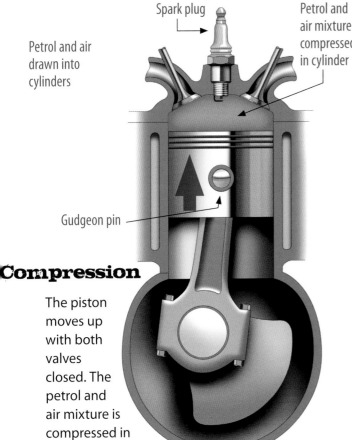

Spark plug

Petrol and air mixture compressed in cylinder

Petrol and air drawn into cylinders

Gudgeon pin

Compression

The piston moves up with both valves closed. The petrol and air mixture is compressed in this tight space.

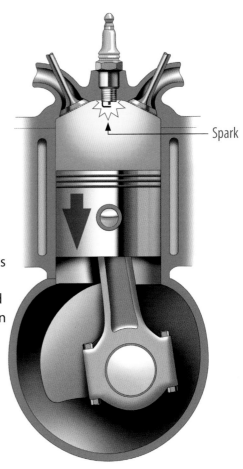

Power

Spark

When the piston is at the top and the petrol and air mixture is compressed, the spark plug ignites the fuel, causing an explosion and forcing the piston down again.

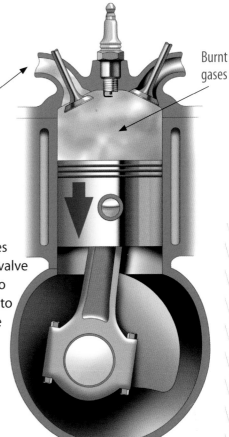

Exhaust valve opens to allow burnt gases to escape into the exhaust pipe

Burnt gases

Exhaust

As the piston moves down the exhaust valve opens via springs to allow burnt gasses to escape out into the exhaust pipe.

FOR YOUR FOLDER

1. What are the four main stages of the four-stroke cycle?

2. During which stage will the spark plug ignite?

3. Briefly explain how the four-stroke cycle works.

4. On what stroke will the inlet valve open?

5. On what stroke will the exhaust valve open?

6. What component causes the inlet valve and exhaust valve to open?

7. What is the name of the component that the piston moves up and down inside?

8. What happens when the mixture of air and petrol burns rapidly on the power stroke?

THE TWO-STROKE CYCLE

(The spark-ignition two-stroke cycle)

Two-stroke engines are much smaller, lighter and cheaper than four-stroke engines. They have no valves like that of a four-stroke and therefore their operation is much simpler.
Two-stroke engines are commonly used in lawnmowers, chainsaws and mopeds.

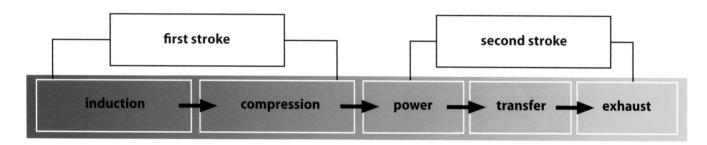

first stroke		second stroke	
induction → compression	power →	transfer →	exhaust

Induction and compression

As the piston moves up the cylinder the inlet valve is uncovered to allow fuel to flow into the cylinder. The piston compresses the fuel from the previous cycle and the spark plug ignites. This causes an explosion, forcing the piston back down.

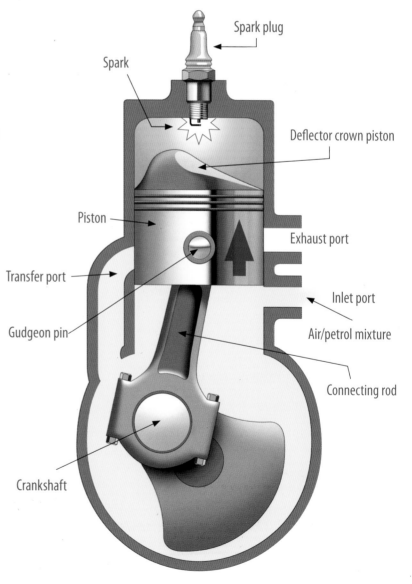

Spark plug

Spark

Deflector crown piston

Piston

Exhaust port

Transfer port

Inlet port

Gudgeon pin

Air/petrol mixture

Connecting rod

Crankshaft

Power, transfer and exhaust

The piston moves down after the explosion, uncovering the exhaust port and the transfer port. As the fuel flows out of the transfer port to the top side of the piston, it pushes the burnt gases out through the exhaust port.

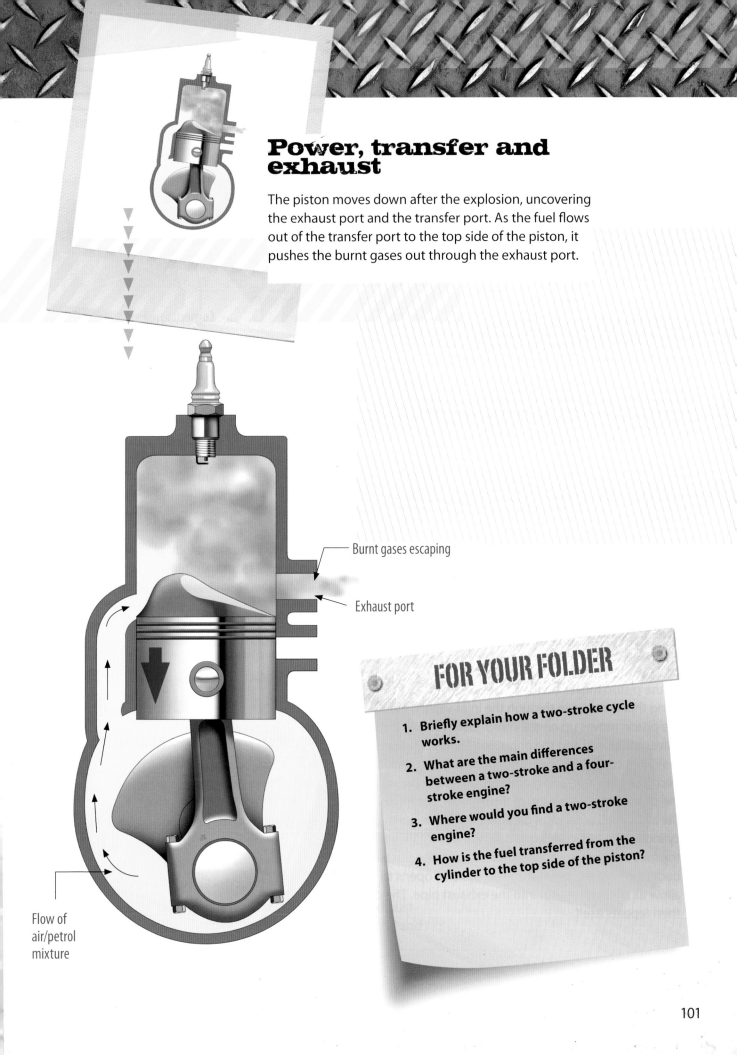

Burnt gases escaping

Exhaust port

Flow of air/petrol mixture

FOR YOUR FOLDER

1. Briefly explain how a two-stroke cycle works.

2. What are the main differences between a two-stroke and a four-stroke engine?

3. Where would you find a two-stroke engine?

4. How is the fuel transferred from the cylinder to the top side of the piston?

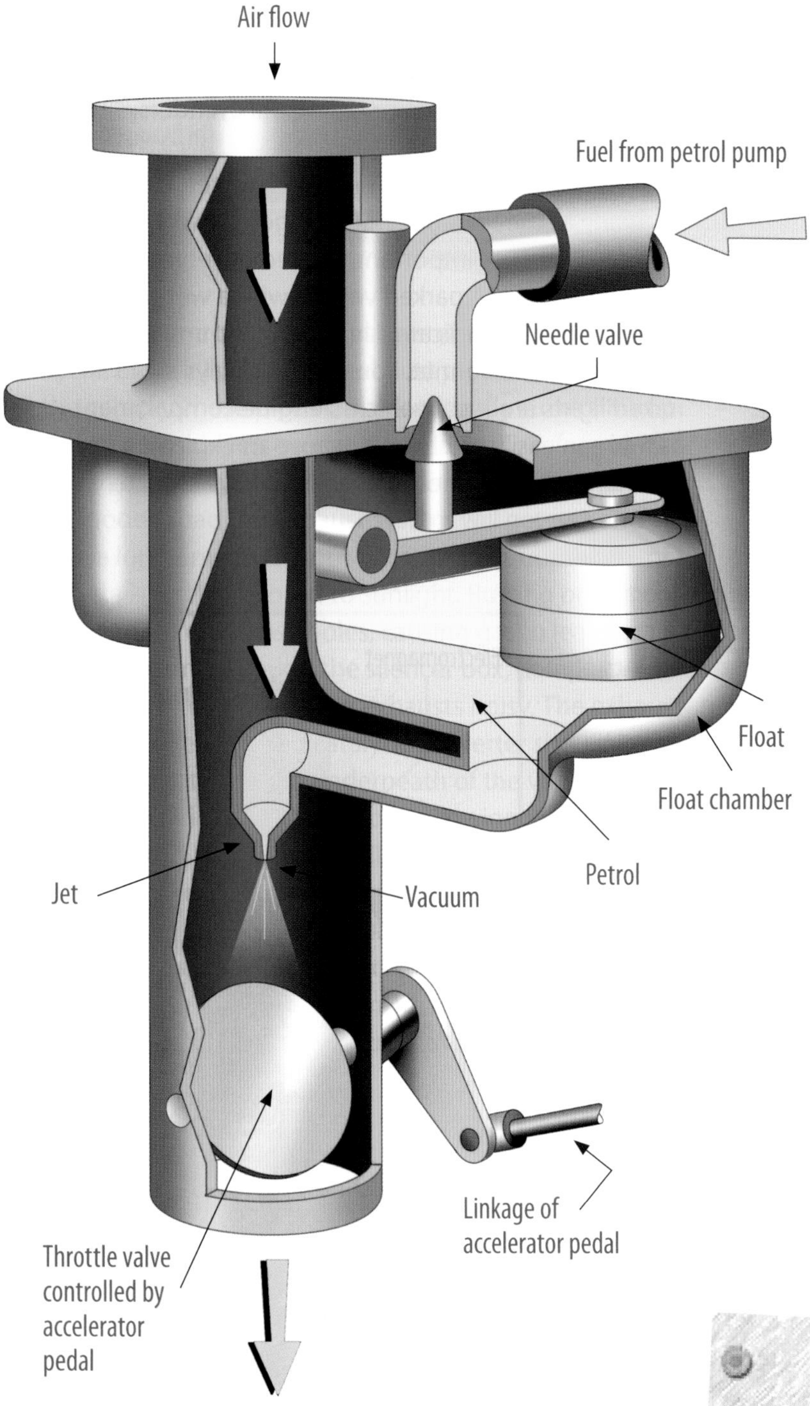

Air flow

Fuel from petrol pump

Needle valve

Jet

Vacuum

Petrol

Float

Float chamber

Throttle valve controlled by accelerator pedal

Linkage of accelerator pedal

Petrol/air mixture moves on into the inlet manifold for each cylinder

The carburettor

The carburettor has two main functions:

- To mix the correct amounts of petrol and air together to make the fuel for burning in cylinders.

- To control the amount of fuel sent to each cylinder.

Petrol flows from the tank at the back of the car, through a petrol pump, to a float chamber in the carburettor. This chamber makes sure that there is a regular, continuous flow of petrol to be mixed with air. When the chamber fills up a float pushes a needle valve into the pipe to stop the flow from the petrol tank.

The venturi is the part of the carburettor that narrows when the petrol and air mix for the first time. A jet is used to ease the flow of petrol out of the pipe line, creating a spray. The air flow then carries the petrol on through to the inlet manifold, that distributes a specific amount of fuel to each of the four cylinders. At this stage the inlet valve will open on the induction stroke, allowing a specific amount of fuel into each cylinder. Whenever the accelerator pedal is pressed the throttle valve opens to allow fuel into the cylinders. The harder the accelerator pedal is pressed the wider the throttle valve opens to allow more fuel into the cylinders.

FOR YOUR FOLDER

1. What is the function of the carburettor?

2. What is the function of the float in the float chamber?

3. What is the venturi?

4. What is the function of the jet?

5. What happens when the accelerator pedal is pressed?

THE TRANSMISSION SYSTEM

The transmission system is used to set a vehicle moving. Its main parts are as follows:

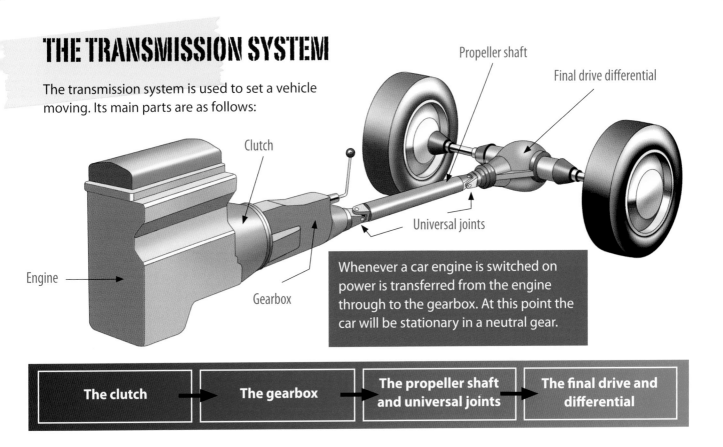

Engine

Clutch

Gearbox

Propeller shaft

Final drive differential

Universal joints

Whenever a car engine is switched on power is transferred from the engine through to the gearbox. At this point the car will be stationary in a neutral gear.

| The clutch | → | The gearbox | → | The propeller shaft and universal joints | → | The final drive and differential |

Although the car is stationary, all the gears inside the gearbox will be rotating. To select a gear to move the vehicle the gears will have to be stopped for a moment. This is achieved by pressing the clutch pedal, which disengages the clutch from the gearbox, stopping all the gears. The gear stick can then be moved to select an appropriate gear. By moving the foot off the clutch pedal it is released and the vehicle will start to move.

The clutch

The main function of the dry friction clutch is to engage (connect) and disengage (disconnect) the engine from the gearbox. By doing this an appropriate gear can be selected.

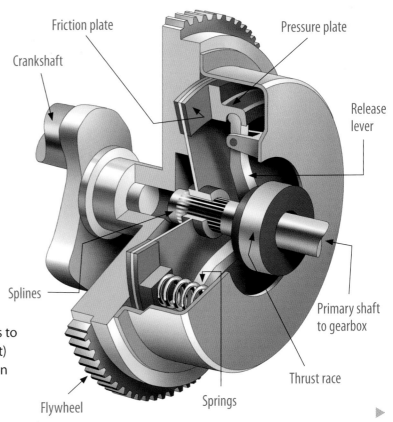

Friction plate

Crankshaft

Pressure plate

Release lever

Primary shaft to gearbox

Thrust race

Splines

Flywheel

Springs

The primary shaft has splines carved into it in certain places to enable the friction plate to slide along the shaft. This slide allows the plate to be forced tight against or moved away from the flywheel. When the clutch is engaged, which is most of the time, the friction plate is forced tight against the flywheel by springs on a pressure plate. The flywheel causes the primary shaft to rotate through to the gearbox.

To disengage the engine from the gearbox the clutch pedal must be pressed and held in. By doing this a linkage mechanism pulls the thrust race, which is connected to the pressure plate. The springs are then compressed allowing the friction plate to move away from the flywheel. When this happens the primary shaft will stop rotating as will the gears in the gearbox.

On releasing the clutch pedal the linkage mechanism releases the springs, which push the pressure plate back against the friction plate, forcing it tight against the flywheel. The primary shaft will once again rotate, as will the gears in the gearbox.

The friction plate is a metal plate that is forced against a metal flywheel. This plate needs protected, therefore both sides of the friction plate are faced (covered) with a special material designed to reduce friction, overheating and wear.

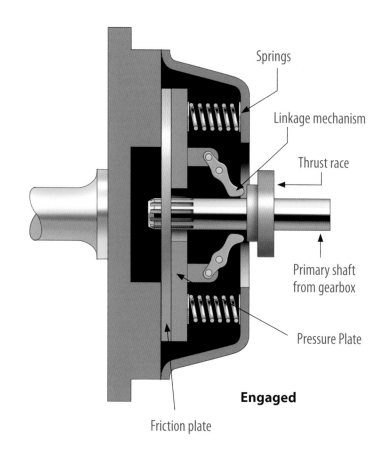

Springs

Linkage mechanism

Thrust race

Primary shaft from gearbox

Pressure Plate

Engaged

Friction plate

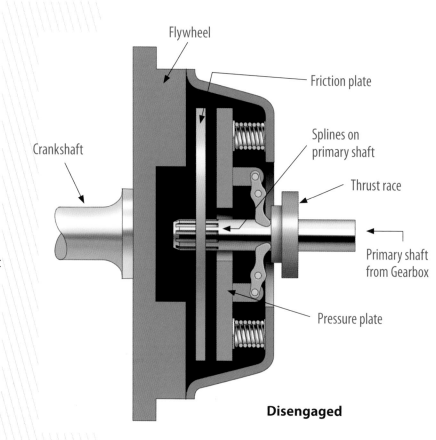

Flywheel

Friction plate

Splines on primary shaft

Thrust race

Primary shaft from Gearbox

Pressure plate

Crankshaft

Disengaged

The gearbox

Most gearboxes have five forward gears and a reverse gear. The gearbox is designed to produce a range of speeds depending on where a vehicle is travelling. For example, high gears are used to increase speed when driving on the flat, whereas driving on an incline or in slow moving traffic require lower gears. Within the transmission system and gearbox lubrication is essential because of the large number of moving parts. This lubricating oil will not only ease the movement of parts but reduce friction, heat and wear.

When a vehicle is switched on power is transmitted from the engine, through the clutch, to the gearbox, which will be in a neutral gear. The primary shaft has one gear that continuously rotates and it is connected to the clutch. When the clutch pedal is pressed by the driver's foot the primary shaft will stop rotating as will all the gears on the layshaft. The layshaft has a number of gears that are permanently fixed from reverse, to first, through to fifth.

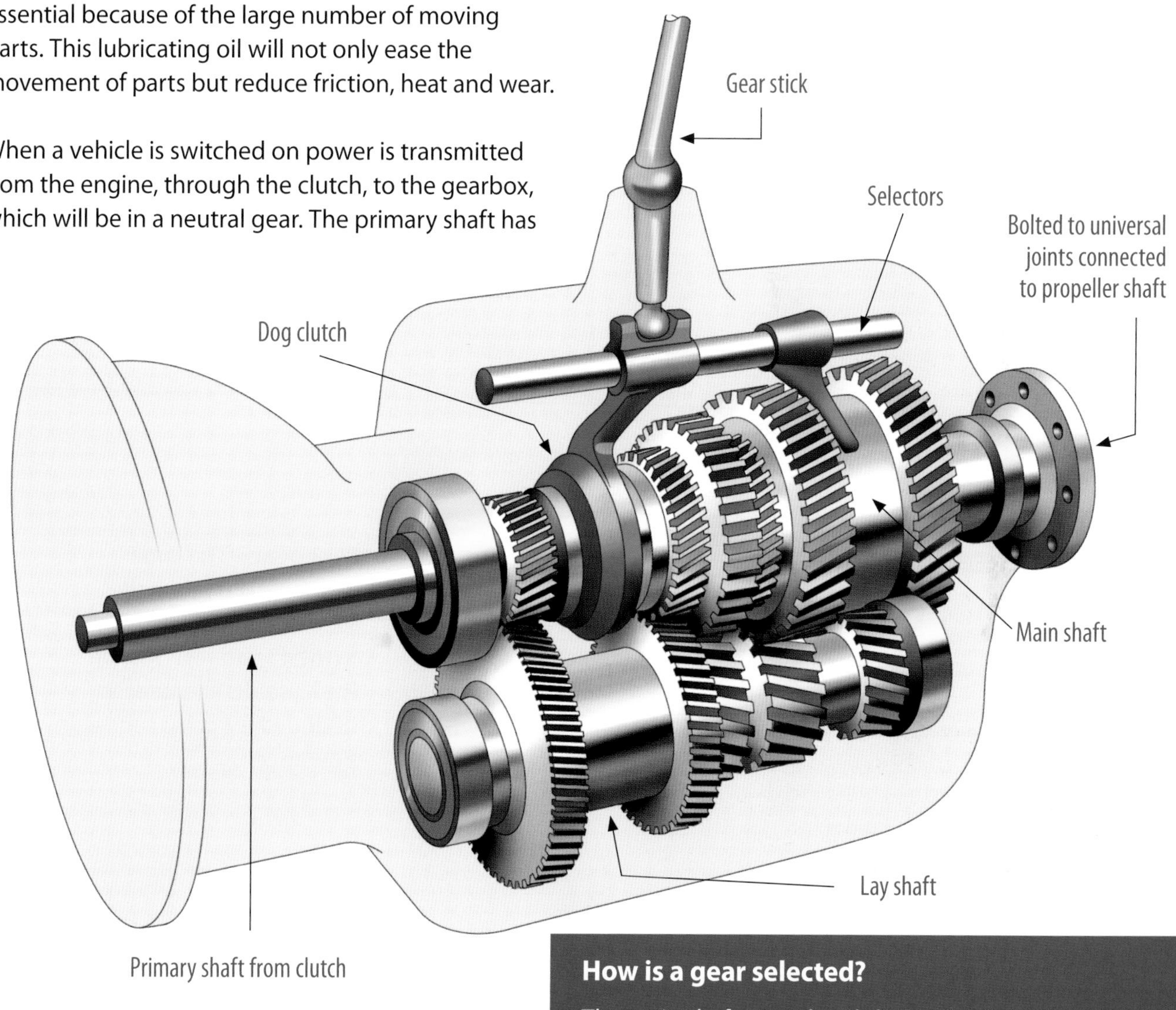

Gear stick

Selectors

Bolted to universal joints connected to propeller shaft

Dog clutch

Main shaft

Lay shaft

Primary shaft from clutch

How is a gear selected?

The main shaft is a splined shaft that allows gears to slide or move from side to side. The gear stick is connected to selectors and dog clutches that slide the gears along the main shaft to engage with gears on the layshaft. This can only happen if all the gears have momentarily been stopped rotating by the clutch, allowing certain gears to be engaged together.

Moving the gear stick without pushing the clutch in will result in a grinding action and the toothed gear wheels could be damaged. The main shaft is connected to a propeller shaft. The propellor shaft transmits the power and motion from the gearbox to the back wheels, which drive the car.

The diagrams below show how the layshaft and main shaft have different gears engaged to provide different speeds for the back wheels. For less speed and more power the gear wheel will be larger. This power is transferred to the back axle from the main shaft.

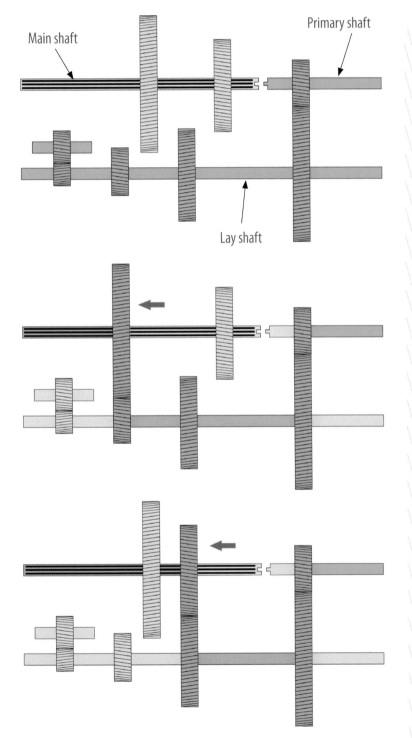

Main shaft

Primary shaft

Lay shaft

Neutral – The small gear on the primary shaft carries power from the engine, through the clutch, to the gearbox. This small gear is permanently meshed with a gear on the layshaft.

First gear – The large gear on the main shaft slides along the splines to mesh with first gear on the layshaft. This gear is designed for power and a slow speed.

Second gear – This gear arrangement has slightly less power, with a slight increase in speed.

Third gear – With the need for more speed the gear on the main shaft will be smaller.

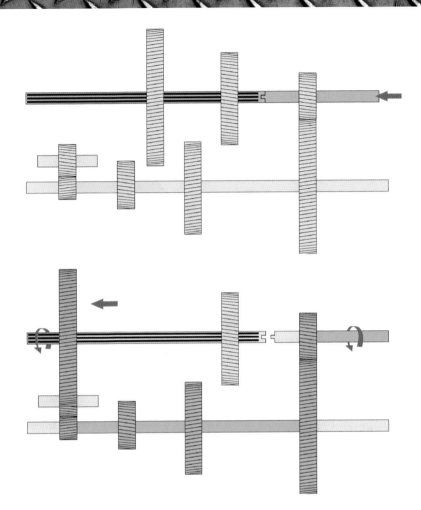

Reverse gear – This uses an idler gear in the middle to turn the main shaft and the layshaft in the same direction.

Calculating gear ratios

Gear ratios are used by vehicle manufacturers to work out either the torque (power) produced by the engine or the speeds at which the vehicle can travel at. Gear ratios are determined by the relationship between the number of teeth that mesh together with another gear.

The calculation to work out gear ratios is very simple.

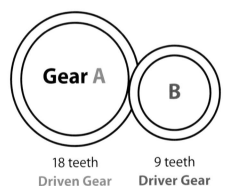

Gear A **B**

18 teeth 9 teeth
Driven Gear **Driver Gear**

To calculate the gear ratio:

$$\text{Gear ratio} = \frac{\text{Number of teeth on driven gear}}{\text{Number of teeth on driver gear}}$$

$$= \frac{18}{9} = \frac{2}{1}$$

Which is written as **Gear Ratio = 2:1**

THE SUSPENSION SYSTEM

When driving on the roads a vehicle may encounter bumps, humps, uneven road surfaces and sometimes potholes. Any of these surfaces can cause bounces or jolts. The function of the suspension system is to reduce and absorb the effects of these surfaces, allowing the vehicle and its occupants to remain in a safe position.

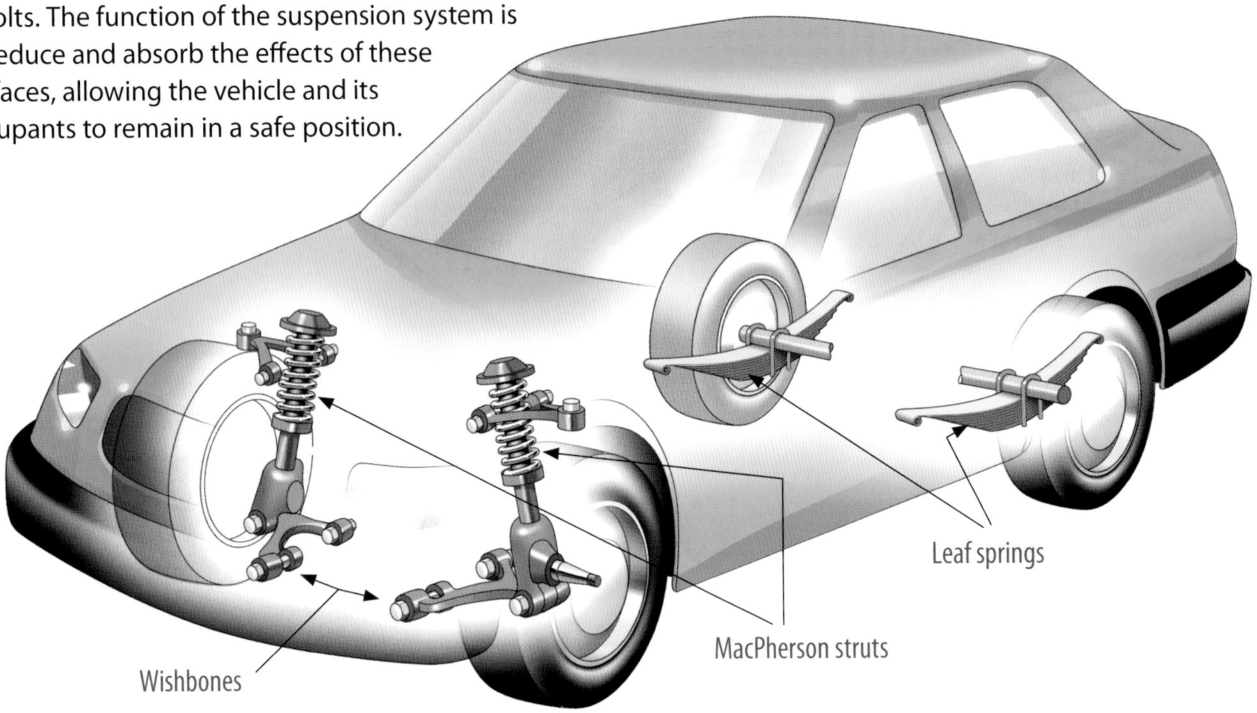

Leaf springs

MacPherson struts

Wishbones

Suspension systems should result in the following:

- A comfortable even journey as the vehicle will absorb the effects of bounces or jolts.

- Less expense and maintenance for the vehicle owner caused by wear and tear, as the vehicle will be shaken about less.

- Easier control and safer handling, because the wheels will always be in contact with the road.

A suspension system is made up of a number of different components for both the front wheels and the back wheels.

Front wheel suspension

The function of the **coil spring** is to absorb the wheels' up and down movement. However, when compressed, a coil can spring back to its original shape at speed. This return action needs to be slowed down. The function of a damper is to slow down the return of a spring.

The **MacPherson strut** is the most common front wheel suspension system. It is made up of a strut, a coil spring and a shock absorber. The strut takes the impact of the wheel striking something, while the shock absorbers slow down the movement of the impact. Each shock absorber uses a piston, which is connected to the suspension system and plunges down into a cylinder of oil, slowing down the movement.

Shock absorbers and dampers can be tested for efficiency by a simple bounce test. To carry out the bounce test you need to press down on one corner of your vehicle at a time. Your vehicle should push down and spring back up again. As it bounces back up it should rise above its starting point and then rest back to its original position. If it drops below this starting point the shock absorber needs replacing. It is important that this check is carried out on each corner.

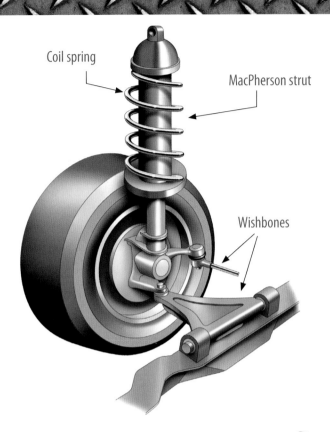

Coil spring

MacPherson strut

Wishbones

Wishbones are a linkage mechanism connected from the car body to the wheels. Its function is to absorb jolts caused by a wheel striking something.

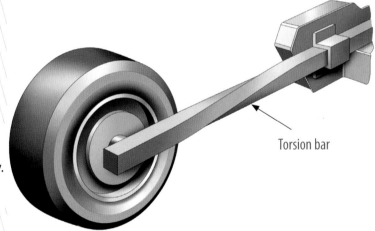

Torsion bar

The **torsion bar**, attached between the frame and the axle, is quite flexible, capable of twisting to absorb shock and maintain stability.

Rear wheel suspension

Leaf springs form part of the rear wheel suspension. They are made up of a number of steel strips sitting on top of each other. As movement occurs the steel strips slide over each other, forcing the wheels back down on the road.

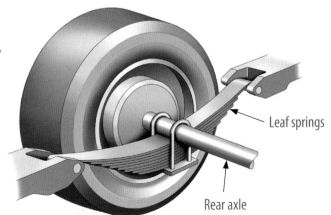

Leaf springs

Rear axle

Viscosity

A viscous liquid is one which is thick and sticky. Oil with a low viscosity is a thin oil and oil with a high viscosity is a thick oil. The SAE (Society of Automotive Engineers) rate and grade oil to find out its level of viscosity. This is done by allowing a measured amount of oil to flow through a set diameter and calculating how long it takes. The longer it takes, the higher the oil's viscosity will be. Oil with a high viscosity will be classified with a high number to identify it as a thick oil.

FOR YOUR FOLDER

1. What is the main function of the lubrication system?

2. What is the meaning of the term viscosity?

3. Where is oil stored?

4. Name two advantages of using oil in an engine?

5. What component is responsible for sending oil around the various parts of the engine?

6. Apart from lubrication what is the main function of oil?

7. Why is it not recommended to move off immediately after starting an engine from cold?

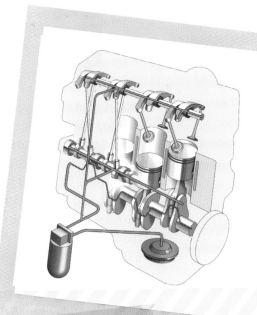

THE COOLING SYSTEM

There are two types of engine cooling systems:

- **Water cooling**
- **Air cooling**

The car engine uses the water cooling system and is surrounded by numerous water passages for the following reasons:

- Water helps to drown out the noise from the engine
- Water helps to keep the engine cool and maintains an even temperature
- The hot water can be used in the car heaters

The two main components for controlling the water temperature of an engine are the thermostat and the pressurised radiator cap. The pistons moving up and down inside the cylinders generate a lot of heat. These cylinders are surrounded by water jackets to help maintain an even temperature around each cylinder. A water pump is used to keep the water circulating around each part. The water pump can be either electrically driven by the battery or mechanically driven. The water pump is connected to the radiator fan, which draws air into the engine. They are connected by pullies and driven by a fan belt, which is turned and rotated by the camshaft, located beside the crankshaft. If the temperature of the water gets too hot a thermostat will detect this. The function of the thermostat is to control the water temperature. When the water gets too hot, the thermostat will open to allow the water to flow through the top hose into a header expansion tank in the top part of the radiator. This header expansion tank is pressurised and allows the water to reach a boiling temperature of 110 degrees Celsius (°C). The radiator is made up of brass cooling fins to increase the cooling surface area. As the water passes from the top of the radiator to the bottom, a fan sucks the cool air in from outside, over the top of the water hoses and cooling fins. This air cools the water, which flows out of the bottom of the radiator through the bottom hose and back into the water jackets around the cylinders.

Water cooling system

The main parts of the water cooling system are:

- *The radiator*
- *The water pump*
- *The thermostat*
- *The water jackets*
- *The heater*

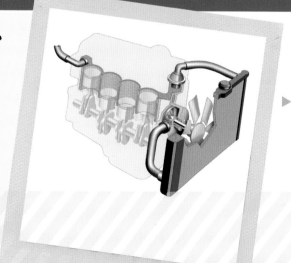

▶▶▶▶▶▶▶▶▶

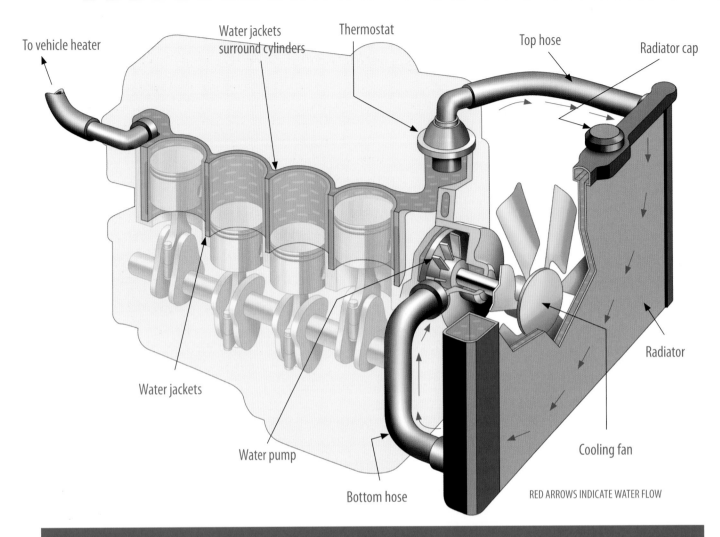

To vehicle heater

Water jackets surround cylinders

Thermostat

Top hose

Radiator cap

Water jackets

Water pump

Bottom hose

Water pump

Cooling fan

Radiator

RED ARROWS INDICATE WATER FLOW

There are a couple of problems associated with the water cooling system. The water can freeze, especially during the winter months, causing the radiator and hoses to burst or the cylinder block to crack. You should put anti-freeze into your engine's water system to prevent it freezing. The recommended level of antifreeze is 30% antifreeze to 70% water.

Leaks can also occur, resulting in reduced water levels and decreased pressure. A shortage of water (coolant) in the radiator will cause the engine to overheat because small amounts of water boil more quickly than large amounts. It is therefore important to frequently check the pipes and hoses; and the water level in the small float tank under the bonnet.

If the water pump fan belt (water pump drive belt) is loose the pump may not be circulating the water down through the radiator and the engine could overheat. You should regularly check the temperature gauge on your vehicle's dashboard

to ensure that the engine's temperature is cool and normal. If you hear your vehicle making a squealing noise it is likely that the fan belt is loose and needs tightened.

Engines run much better when they are warm (a temperature between 85 and 110 °C). Water usually boils at a temperature of 100 °C, therefore the water in the engine is extremely hot. A pressurised radiator cap is positioned at the top of the radiator to seal it and pressurise the water. A spring valve is fitted underneath this cap. If the temperature rises too high or the pressure becomes too great the valve releases the built up pressure by allowing water back into the expansion tank. The water will not boil until it is about 110 °C. If the temperature rises much more than this the engine could overheat causing serious damage and the radiator could even burst. A sign of a vehicle overheating is steam blowing out from under the bonnet, coming from the engine.

Air cooling system

Air cooling systems are mainly used on motorcycles and mopeds. The water cooling system has cooling fins on the radiator. In the air cooling system the fins are directly connected to the cylinders to increase the cooling surfaces. A thermostat detects the engine overheating and therefore reacts by opening a flap to allow air in from the atmosphere. A fan in the engine circulates the air over the fins and around the cylinders to reduce the temperature. Once the temperature is reduced the thermostat closes the flap to stop air flowing into the engine, allowing it to warm up again. To get the best air flow this system works much better when the vehicle is moving. The air cooling system has a number of advantages: it is lighter than the water cooling system as it does not have to use or store water, and there is no water to leak or freeze. However, the air cooling system's main disadvantage is that it can be noisy. The water cooling system uses the water to help drown out engine noise.

FOR YOUR FOLDER

7. What is the main purpose of the radiator cap?

8. Why is the cooling system pressurised?

9. Name the component in the cooling system which opens automatically when the engine gets too hot.

10. What damage can happen to an engine's cooling system if anti-freeze is not added to it during the winter months?

FOR YOUR FOLDER

1. Name three advantages of the water cooling system.

2. Why are the main parts of the water cooling system surrounded by water?

3. What is the function of the radiator?

4. How is the speed of water circulation increased?

5. Name the main parts of the water cooling system?

6. What is the purpose of the thermostat?

THE BRAKING SYSTEM

The braking system is one of the most important systems within a motor vehicle. It is essential that all vehicles have good brakes to ensure the safety of the occupants and other road users. Needed for slowing down, stopping and control, it is important that all vehicles have the following two braking systems:

- **The mechanical system (the handbrake)**   *for parking*
  rear wheels only

- **The hydraulic system**   *to slow down and stop a vehicle*
  (A) front wheels – disc brakes } *all four wheels*
  (B) rear wheels – drum brakes

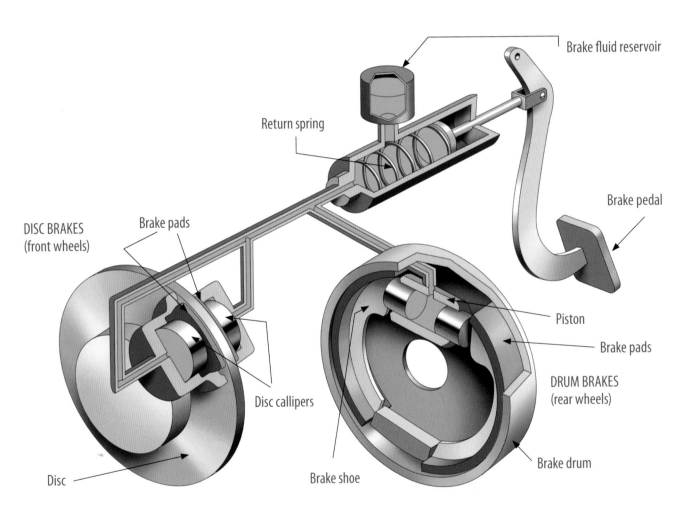

Brake fluid reservoir

Return spring

Brake pedal

DISC BRAKES
(front wheels)

Brake pads

Piston

Brake pads

DRUM BRAKES
(rear wheels)

Disc callipers

Brake drum

Disc

Brake shoe

mechanical = levers + pullys
hydrolic = fluid ~ glows through tubes to pressurise
break fluid has higher viscosity

Main parts of the braking system

Brake pedal – This is a foot-operated lever inside the vehicle, which is used to slow down or stop the vehicle by operating on all its four wheels.

Brake master cylinder – This main cylinder draws the brake fluid from a small tank found under the bonnet. It uses a piston to force the brake fluid through pipelines to each wheel when the brake pedal is pressed.

The brake servo – This unit determines how much brake pressure has been applied by the foot and allows the required amounts of brake fluid to flow to each wheel, slowing down or stopping the vehicle when needed.

Brake pipes – These pipes connect all four wheels from the brake pedal and master cylinder. The brake fluid flows through these pipes to all four wheels.

Brake shoes – Brake shoes are the part of the brake mechanism that moves towards the rotating wheels, slowing down or stopping the vehicle when the brake pedal is pressed. They also move away from the wheel when the brake pedal is released.

Slave/wheel cylinders – These cylinders are present in each wheel and contain pistons, which are connected to the brake shoes. The pistons are forced out by brake fluid to move the shoes against the rotating drums.

Brake drums – The wheels of the vehicle are connected to the brake drums. The drums rotate when the wheels rotate.

Disc callipers – These are strong metal casings that are only found on the disc brakes, on the front wheels. They are used to hold brake pads in place either side of a rotating steel disc that is connected to the wheels.

Disc/brake pads – The brake pads are lined on top of the brake shoes within the drum brakes. They are pressed and rub against the rotating drum, causing friction to slow down and eventually stop the vehicle. Within disc brakes, the pads are located either side of the steel disc and produce a pinching action when pressed against the disc, again causing friction to slow down or stop the vehicle.

Handbrake – This is a lever-operated brake found inside the vehicle. It is used for parking and is only applied on the back brakes.

The hydraulic braking system consists of brake pads that are connected to the wheel cylinder. These cylinders are filled with brake fluid, which forces the pads against the discs or drums, causing the wheels to slow down. The level of this fluid can be checked under the bonnet. A small dipstick is attached to the cap of the brake fluid reservoir to check the level of brake fluid. It is important that the correct level of brake fluid is present to ensure that the brakes function properly. Brake pads generate friction and heat because they rub against a rotating disc or drum. These pads will eventually wear thin and will need to be replaced by a mechanic to restore the effectiveness of the braking. The hydraulic system's action is quiet, with few parts to wear and only the brake pads needing to be replaced.

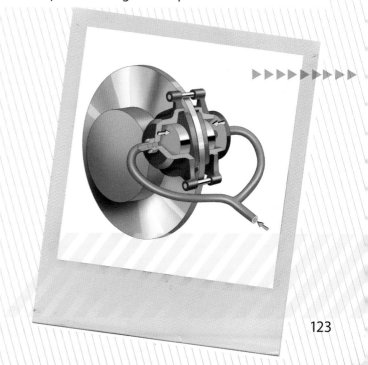

Disc brakes

These brakes are usually found only on the front wheels. The wheel is bolted on and connected to the brake disc. On pressing the brake pedal a piston in the master cylinder pushes the brake fluid along pipelines to force the brake pads, which are on either side, in against the rotating disc. The pressure applied causes a pinching action and will determine how quickly the discs stop rotating. On releasing the brake pedal a spring forces the piston back into the master cylinder. The brake fluid pressure is then reduced, releasing the force applied on the pads against the discs.

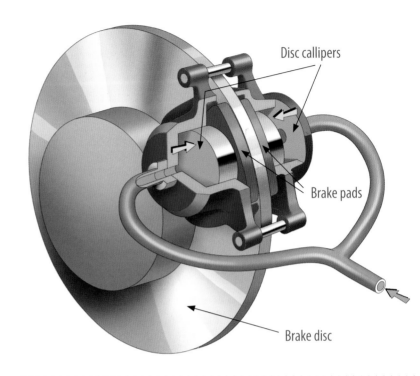

Disc callipers

Brake pads

Brake disc

Drum brakes

The wheel is bolted to a drum that rotates. When the brake pedal is pressed, a piston in the master cylinder pushes brake fluid along pipelines to hydraulic cylinders contained inside the brake drum. These hydraulic cylinders have pistons connected to brake shoes that are lined with pads. The pistons force these shoes with pads out against the rotating drum, causing it to slow down and eventually stop. The springs inside the drum that hold the brake shoes and pads away from the rotating drum are also extended. On releasing the brake pedal the springs return to their original state, pulling the brake shoes and pads away from the drum, allowing the wheels to rotate again.

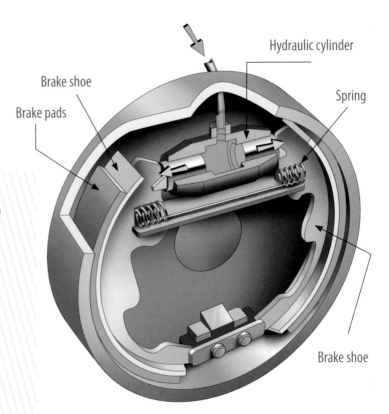

Brake shoe

Brake pads

Hydraulic cylinder

Spring

Brake shoe

The mechanical system

The mechanical braking system only applies to the operation of the handbrake. The handbrake is applied by hand on the driver's left hand side. It is only applied on the rear drum brakes and is used when parking or sitting stationary for a period of time, such as waiting at traffic lights.

Anti-lock braking system (ABS)

ABS stands for anti-lock braking system. This system is fitted to most modern cars. Each wheel has special sensors that detect a locking brake. This system uses a pumping action of applying, releasing and reapplying pressure on the brakes. This pinching action is carried out on each wheel to keep control of the vehicle and to prevent skidding. The vehicle should safely come to a halt.

FOR YOUR FOLDER

1. Why is the braking system considered to be the primary safety feature in a vehicle?
2. Briefly explain the function of the brakes.
3. Name two braking systems in a motor vehicle.
4. What does ABS stand for?
5. Name an advantage of the ABS braking system.
6. Briefly explain how ABS brakes work.
7. On what wheels do the hydraulic braking system operate?
8. Name two types of brakes used in the hydraulic braking system.
9. Briefly explain how drum brakes work.
10. Where on a vehicle would you find disc brakes?

INDEX

H

Handbrake 51, 82, 122, 125
Harness 55
Hazard 17, 19, 27, 31, 34, 81
Hazard warning plates 6, 14
Headlights 24–25, 27–28, 30–31
Head restraints 41
Headwinds 29, 31
Heater 89, 119–120
Helmet 24, 36, 56, 75
Henry Ford 60
HGV 49
Hidden dip 22
High-sided vehicle 29, 31
High tension leads 93
Highway Code 6–7, 9–10, 12, 14, 16–18, 20, 27, 33, 37, 40, 42, 55, 64, 69
Hire purchase 72
Hit and run 81
Horizontal deflection 39, 64
Hose 119–120
Hydraulic braking system 123, 125
Hydrocarbons 66, 103

I

Ice 24, 29, 31
Ignite 93–94, 96–97, 99–100, 102–103, 105
Ignition 82
Ignition switch 93
Ignition system 91, 93–94
Impact 41, 56, 61, 65, 85, 87, 114, 131–132
Impair 19, 26, 32, 34–35, 38, 66
Incised wounds 85
Indemnity 45
Indemnity fee 77–78
Inducements 74
Induction 98, 100, 102, 106
Injection 56, 102
Injury 21, 37, 43, 55, 83
Inlet manifold 105–106
Inlet valve 96, 98–100, 102, 106
Insurance 44–49, 52, 69–71, 73, 80–81
Interest 72–75, 78–79
Interest rates 73
Internal combustion engine 59–60, 98

J

Jetstyle helmet 56
Jump leads 25
Junction 11, 18, 27, 38

K

Karl Benz 59, 60
Knock for knock 45

L

Lacerated wound 85
Law 7, 9, 27, 32, 42, 59, 68–70
Layshaft 109–111
Leaf springs 114–115
Leasing 73
Legal requirements 6, 9, 36–37, 44–47, 49, 52, 55, 73
Legislation 67, 69
Licence 33, 46, 48–50, 52, 69, 70, 73
Lighting components 92
Lighting up times 27
Linkage 108, 115
Loading restrictions 14
Loans 72–73
Low sun 26
LRP 67–68
Lubrication 96, 109, 117–118

M

MacPherson strut 114–116
Maintenance 41, 74, 114
Manoeuvres 7, 18–19, 24, 28, 34–36, 38, 42
Manufacturers 60–61, 67–68, 71
Mass production 60
Mechanical braking system 125
Mileage 72, 75
Mobility vehicle 35
Monthly repayments 72, 78
Moped 42, 48, 100, 112, 121
MOT 7, 26, 49, 51–52, 70–75
MOT certificate 49, 51, 71, 75
Motorcycle 29, 54, 56–57, 59, 69, 112, 121
Motoring laws 68–70
Motoring costs 72–75
Motoring mathematics 71–79
Motorway 6, 8, 10, 13, 15, 19, 28–29, 31, 33, 40–41, 60, 62–63, 82
Mouth-to mouth 83

N

National speed limit 39–40
NCPS 36–37
Neutral 107, 109–110
Newly qualified driver 49, 73
Nitrogen oxide 66–67
No claims bonus 45, 47, 80

GLOSSARY

Green card – motorists will need to produce this document to enable them to drive in countries outside the EU.

Gudgeon pin – a pin that connects the piston to the connecting rod.

Hazard – anything that causes an obstruction or is a danger to a road user.

Headwind – wind that slows down the movement of road users, especially affecting cyclists, motorcyclists and pedestrians.

Hidden dip – a dangerous part of the road where traffic may be concealed in a dip in the road while a motorist thinks they can see an entire, clear stretch of road ahead.

Hire purchase – a method of borrowing money from a finance company.

Horizontal deflection – a traffic calming measure used to slow down the speed of motorists.

Hydrocarbons – a pollutant found in exhaust emissions.

Incised wounds – these are open, cut wounds, usually made by a sharp instrument.

Indemnity – compensation from insurance companies restoring a person's financial position after an incident has occurred.

Inducements – special offers made to regular customers.

Induction – the drawing of fuel or air into a cylinder.

Inlet manifold – the part of the fuel system which distributes fuel to the individual cylinders.

Internal combustion engine – any engine that operates by burning fuel inside the engine.

Lacerated wounds – these are caused by impact, resulting in a crushing of bones, and a ripping and tearing of flesh.

Leaf springs – these are steel strips mounted on top of each other, which are found in rear wheel suspension systems.

Leasing – effectively the renting of a vehicle, through monthly payments.

Lighting up times – times when street and vehicle lights are supposed to be switched on.

MacPherson strut – the most commonly used front wheel suspension system.

Mass production – large quantities of the same product manufactured.

Mechanical braking system – the operation of the handbrake.

NCPS – a programme set up in primary schools to educate children in cycling safety.

No claims bonus – a percentage reduction in the cost of insurance for having made no claims.

Pedestrianisation zone – an area that is free from vehicles allowing pedestrians to move around freely.

Peripheral vision – refers to your side vision, an ability to see things outside your direct line of sight.

Personal liability – Accepting responsibility for causing a road accident and what you are personally responsible for paying.

Policy holder/proposer/first party – this is any motorist with or looking for insurance.

Power steering – a system that allows the wheels to be turned without any real force.

Premium – the price you have to pay for insurance cover.

Primary safety – relates to the features that help a vehicle to perform safely under everyday driving conditions.

Proposer/first party/policy holder/ – this is any motorist with or looking for insurance.

Punctured wound – these are open wounds caused by something sharp piercing the skin.

Recovery position – to place someone onto his or her side, with the chin forward and the hand underneath the cheek. This position is used if a casualty is unconscious to tilt the mouth downwards, allowing any fluids to drain out of the mouth and to prevent a casualty from swallowing the tongue.

Renewal notice – a notice sent out by the insurance company to state that your insurance is about to expire. It will include a new start date and the cost for the next term.

Road studs – these help motorists to identify their road position in the dark. There are four different colours of studs: amber, red, green and white.

Running costs – the day-to-day costs of owning a motor vehicle.

SORN document – a legal document to state that a vehicle is being kept off the road, without tax.

Safe grip – a coloured surface material on the road which provides additional grip to vehicles, helping them slow down more safely. It is also used on cycle tracks or at the entrance to residential areas to indicate a 30 mph speed limit.

Second party/broker – the insurance company or insurance company's representative selling the insurance.

Side impact bars – a feature of secondary safety, these bars are inserted into the door panels of a vehicle to improve passenger protection

Silencer box – located in the exhaust system it reduces noise pollution by slowing down the airflow, lowering gas pressures and therefore noise.

Spark plugs – these provide a spark to ignite the fuel in the engine.

Speed cushions – a traffic calming measure used to encourage reduced vehicle speeds.

Stimulant – a drug or liquid that makes you feel happy and more confident, affecting your awareness and reaction times.

Straight sale – the buying of a vehicle without trading another in against it.

Sump – located at the bottom of the engine where oil is stored.

Thermostat – part of the water cooling system used to control the temperature of the water around the engine.

Third party – any person or road user other than the driver who has been involved in an accident.

Third party insurance – this type of insurance covers the driver if they damage the property of or injure a third party while driving. It does not cover any damage caused to the driver or vehicle they are driving.

Third party fire and theft – this type of insurance is exactly the same as third party, with the additional benefit that it also allows the driver to claim if the car is stolen or set on fire.

Tunnel vision – the loss of peripheral vision, where the focus is circular and restricted.

Underwriter – an insurance company employee who makes a risk assessment and decides whether or not to accept an insurance proposal.

Universal joints – part of the transmission system that allows flexibility of the drive or propeller shaft, allowing for circular and up and down movements.

Utmost good faith – the description of a person who has acted honestly with regards to an insurance claim.

Viscosity – a term used to describe the quality and characteristics of different types of oil.

GLOSSARY

Vulnerable road users – the young, the elderly, the disabled and non-motorised road users are all more vulnerable on the road than vehicle drivers who are fit and able. This is because of their inexperience, physical restrictions or lack of a safety framework protecting them.

Warranties – a guarantee, which often comes with new vehicles, covering the cost of repair for vehicle faults and malfunctions during a specified period of time.

Water jackets – these are water passages that surround the cylinders in an engine to help maintain an even temperature.

Water pump – the part of the water cooling system that keeps the water circulating around the engine.